AF344566

kestnergesellschaft   KEHRER

ONE HUNDRED FISH FOUNTAIN Bruce Nauman

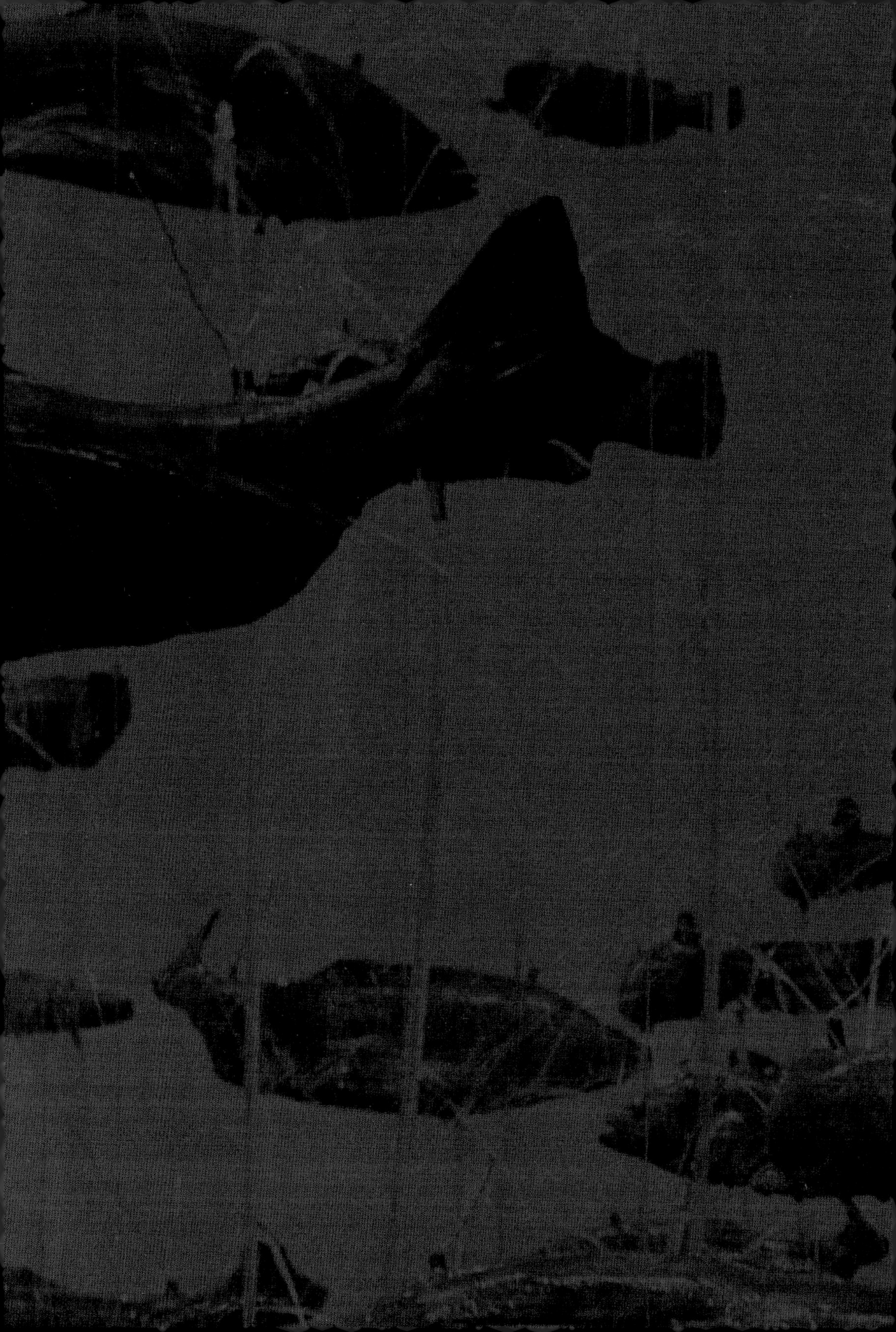

Inhalt

Content

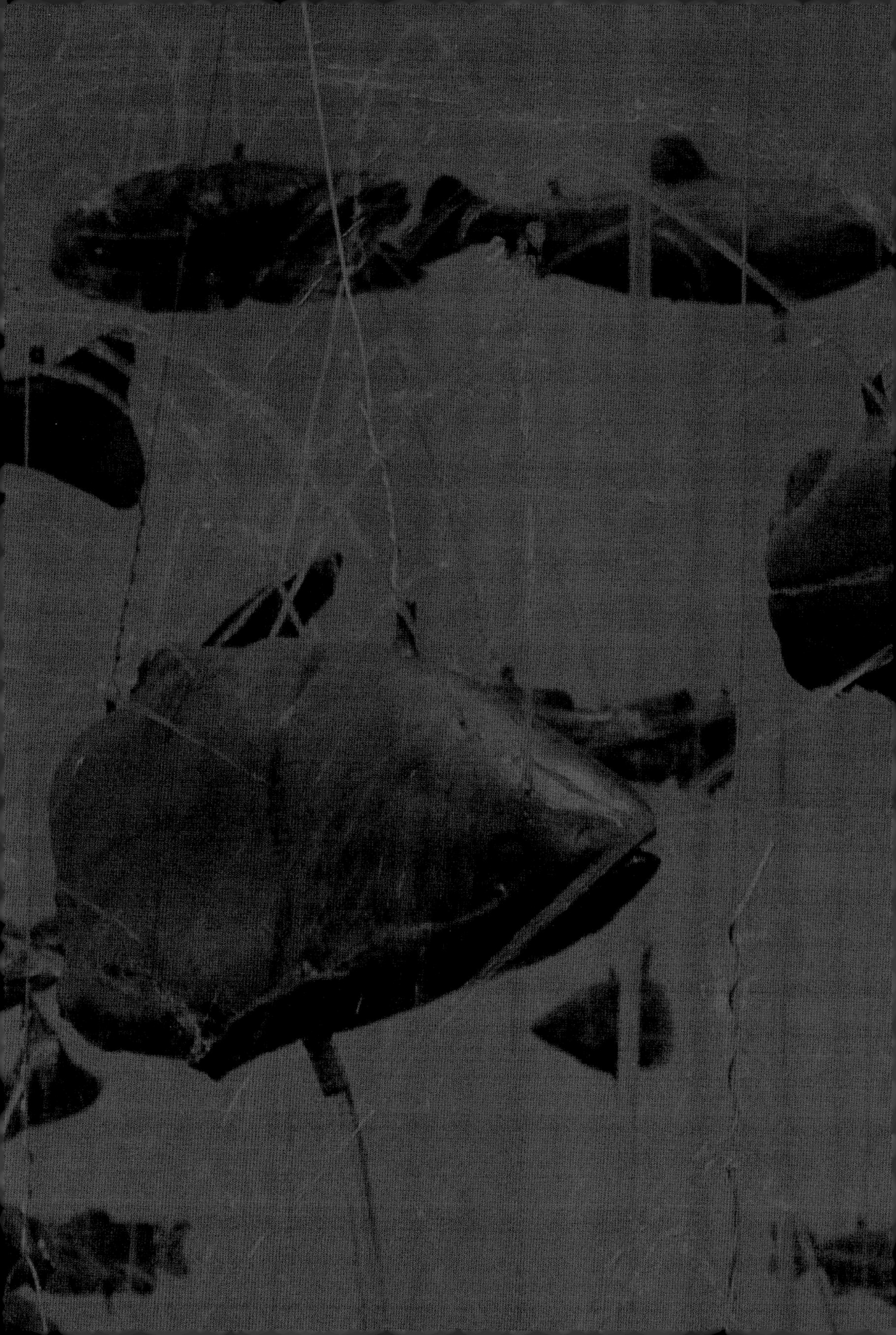

Das Geschenk der Fische

VEIT GÖRNER

The Gift of the Fish

»Ich hatte auch die Vorstellung, dass alles, was ich tat, wenn ich mich in meinem Atelier aufhielt, Kunst war: zum Beispiel das Umhergehen. Wie bringt man das aber in ein Gefüge, damit man es als Kunst präsentieren kann?« ▸ *Bruce Nauman im Interview mit Joan Simon 1987* .... Bei diesem Statement zu seinen frühen Arbeiten wird deutlich, dass für Nauman Kunst ihre ureigenste Berechtigung aus dem realen Leben ableitet. Dabei interessieren ihn weniger die Sensationen als vielmehr die Beiläufigkeiten: das Gehen im Atelier, die endlose Wiederholung eines Wortes bis zur Erschöpfung oder die plastische Darstellung des Sprichworts »Von der Hand in den Mund«. Ähnlich wie Samuel Beckett seziert er die Wirklichkeit, sieht hinter die Offensichtlichkeit der Dinge und versucht für das Selbstverständliche, auch für das Selbstverständliche des Geringsten, eine künstlerische Form zu finden, die es aus ihrem realen Kontext herauslöst und das zeigt, was man nicht sieht oder übersieht oder anders sieht. Als die concept art in den 1960er Jahren Fragen nach dem Verhältnis zwischen Realität und ihrer sprachlichen oder bildhaften Repräsentation aufwarf, wie zum Beispiel Joseph Kosuth mit seiner Arbeit *One and*

»I also had the idea that everything I did when I was in my studio was art: for example, simply walking around. But how do you structure something like that in order to be able to present it as art?« ▸ *Bruce Nauman in an interview with Joan Simon, 1987* .... This statement about his early works makes it clear that for Bruce Nauman, art derives its deepest raison d'être from real life. What interests him in this regard are not so much physical sensations but rather incidental events: walking around his studio, the endless repetition of a word to the point of exhaustion, or the plastic representation of the saying »from hand to mouth.« Just like Samuel Beckett, Nauman dissects reality, opens up a view behind the apparent reality of things, and endeavors to find for that which goes without saying, for the self-evidence of even the most minor matters, an artistic form which removes them from their real context and presents those aspects which one does not see or sees differently. When in the nineteen-sixties Concept Art raised questions concerning the relationship between reality and its linguistic or pictorial representation – for instance Joseph Kosuth with his work *One and Three Chair* (1965), in which a real chair was combined with its photograph and a definition of the word »chair« –, Nauman was

Three Chair (1965), bei der er einen realen Stuhl mit einer Fotografie dieses Stuhls und einer Definition des Wortes »Stuhl« kombinierte, interessierte Nauman vielmehr das Volumen unter dem Stuhl. Der Raum, der zwischen Sitzfläche, Fußboden und den vier Stuhlbeinen definiert wird; das Nichts, das sich trotz allem in seinen Begrenzungen definieren lässt ....
Bruce Nauman zählt seit über 25 Jahren konstant zu den wichtigsten Künstlern weltweit. Wie kein anderer hat er sein Œuvre in konzentrischen Kreisen in den unterschiedlichsten Medien ausgeweitet: Zeichnung, Skulptur, Video und Installationen. Wie kein anderer ist er in seiner spröden Vielschichtigkeit bis heute zum Vorbild nachfolgender Künstlergenerationen geworden. Und wie nur Wenige wurde er seit 1968 fünfmal zur documenta nach Kassel eingeladen ....
Es ist uns eine besondere Ehre, seine neueste große skulpturale Installation *One Hundred Fish Fountain* nach Stationen bei der Dia: Beacon, USA und im Musée d'Art Contemporain de Montréal, Kanada als erstes Haus in Europa und als Einziges in Deutschland zeigen zu können. Ich danke Bruce Nauman für

much more interested in the volume beneath the chair: the space which is delineated between sitting surface, floor and the four legs of the chair; that nothingness which, in spite of everything, may be defined in terms of its limits ....
For more than twenty-five years now, Bruce Nauman has been constantly numbered among the most important artists worldwide. Like no one else, he has extended his oeuvre outward in concentric circles into the most highly varied media: drawing, sculpture, video and installation. His uncompromising diversity has made him a role model for subsequent generations of artists right down to the present. And like only a few other colleagues, he has been invited five times since 1968 to the documenta in Kassel ....
It is a special honor for the kestnergesellschaft, as the first institution in Europe and the only house in Germany, to present his most recent large sculptural installation, *One Hundred Fish Fountain*, after it's showings at the Dia:Beacon in the USA and the Musée d'Art Contemporain de Montréal, Canada. I would like to express my heartfelt thanks to Bruce Nauman for agreeing to this exhibition, and especially to his assistant of many years, Juliet Myers, for her conscientious attentiveness to matters large and small; for the extensive

sein Einverständnis und besonders seiner langjährigen Assistentin Juliet Myers, die mir schon für die große Bruce Nauman Ausstellung im Kunstmuseum Wolfsburg eine unverzichtbare Hilfe war, für ihre gewissenhafte Begleitung..

Sehr dankbar bin ich ebenso Donald Young, der bei der Tourneeplanung für diese außerordentliche Arbeit an uns gedacht und uns vor Anderen den Vorzug gegeben hat. Die Zusammenarbeit mit dem Team seiner Galerie, allen voran Emily Letourneau und Brennan McGaffey, dem Cheftechniker, ohne den der Aufbau dieser komplexen Installation nicht möglich gewesen wäre, war sehr professionell und sehr freundschaftlich. Auch dafür meinen herzlichen Dank...

Besonders hervorzuheben sind jedoch Lenore und Adam Sender, die uns nicht nur als Leihgeber die Arbeit zur Verfügung gestellt haben, sondern auch als Förderer einen maßgeblichen Anteil an der Realisierung des Kataloges geleistet haben. Dafür möchte ich mich ganz herzlich bedanken und Todd Levin, Kurator der Sender Collection, für seine Moderation und Unterstützung mit einschließen...

Bruce Nauman exhibition in the Kunstmuseum Wolfsburg, her assistance already proved to be indispensable for me ....

I am likewise very thankful to Donald Young who, when planning the tour for this extraordinary work, thought of our institution and gave us precedence over others. We have enjoyed an utterly professional and friendly collaboration with the team from his gallery, above all Emily Letourneau and Brennan McGaffey, the chief technician without whom it would not have been possible to set up this complex installation. My sincere thanks to all these individuals as well..

And well worthy of a special expression of gratitude are Lenore and Adam Sender, who not only as lenders have made the work available to us, but also as patrons have made a fundamental contribution to the realization of the catalogue. For that twofold generosity I would like to voice my heartfelt thanks to him, and also to Todd Levin, the curator of the Sender Collection, for his moderatorship and support...............

I am also indebted to the *NORD/LB* whose financial support made this exhibition possible. For many years

Zu sehr großem Dank bin ich auch der *NORD/LB* verpflichtet, die mit ihrer finanziellen Förderung die Ausstellung ermöglicht hat. Seit langem ist die *Norddeutsche Landesbank* für die kestnergesellschaft ein ganz wichtiger und zuverlässiger Partner...
Sandra Grant-Marchand und Anne-Marie Zeppetelli, unsere Kolleginnen aus Montréal haben maßgeblich mitgewirkt, die großvolumige Installation in nur sehr kurzer Zeit und mit exaktem Timing zwischen allen Beteiligten rechtzeitig nach Hannover zu bringen. Ein großer Dank dafür nach Montréal...............
Ohne die großzügige Unterstützung des Förderkreises der kestnergesellschaft hätten wir von der Durchführung dieser grandiosen Präsentation Abstand nehmen müssen. Ein großer Dank dafür ....
Last but not least danke ich Frank-Thorsten Moll, nicht nur für sein kuratorisches Engagement, sondern, vor allem für die Realisierung des begleitenden Ausstellungskataloges und seinen erläuternden Text, der sich trefflich mit den Gedanken von Roland Meyer ergänzt. Es ist die erste wissenschaftliche Publikation zu dieser Arbeit und damit ein weiteres Privileg für die kestnergesellschaft..

the *Norddeutsche Landesbank* has been a very important and reliable partner to the kestnergesellschaft.
Sandra Grant-Marchand and Anne-Marie Zeppetelli, our colleagues in Montréal, were of essential help in bringing this large-volumed installation punctually to Hannover, with astounding speed and exact timing among all the participants. Our deep thanks go accordingly to Montréal...
Without the generous support of the Friends of the kestnergesellschaft, we would have had to decline mournfully the opportunity to realize this outstanding presentation. Heartfelt thanks for this contribution to the success of the project...
Last but not least, I would like to commend Frank-Thorsten Moll, not only for his first-rate curatorial involvement, but also – with particular emphasis – for the realization of the catalogue accompanying the exhibition, as well as for his elucidating text, which is splendidly complemented by the thoughts of Roland Meyer. The catalogue is the first scholarly publication concerning this work and hence constitutes a further privilege for the kestnergesellschaft...

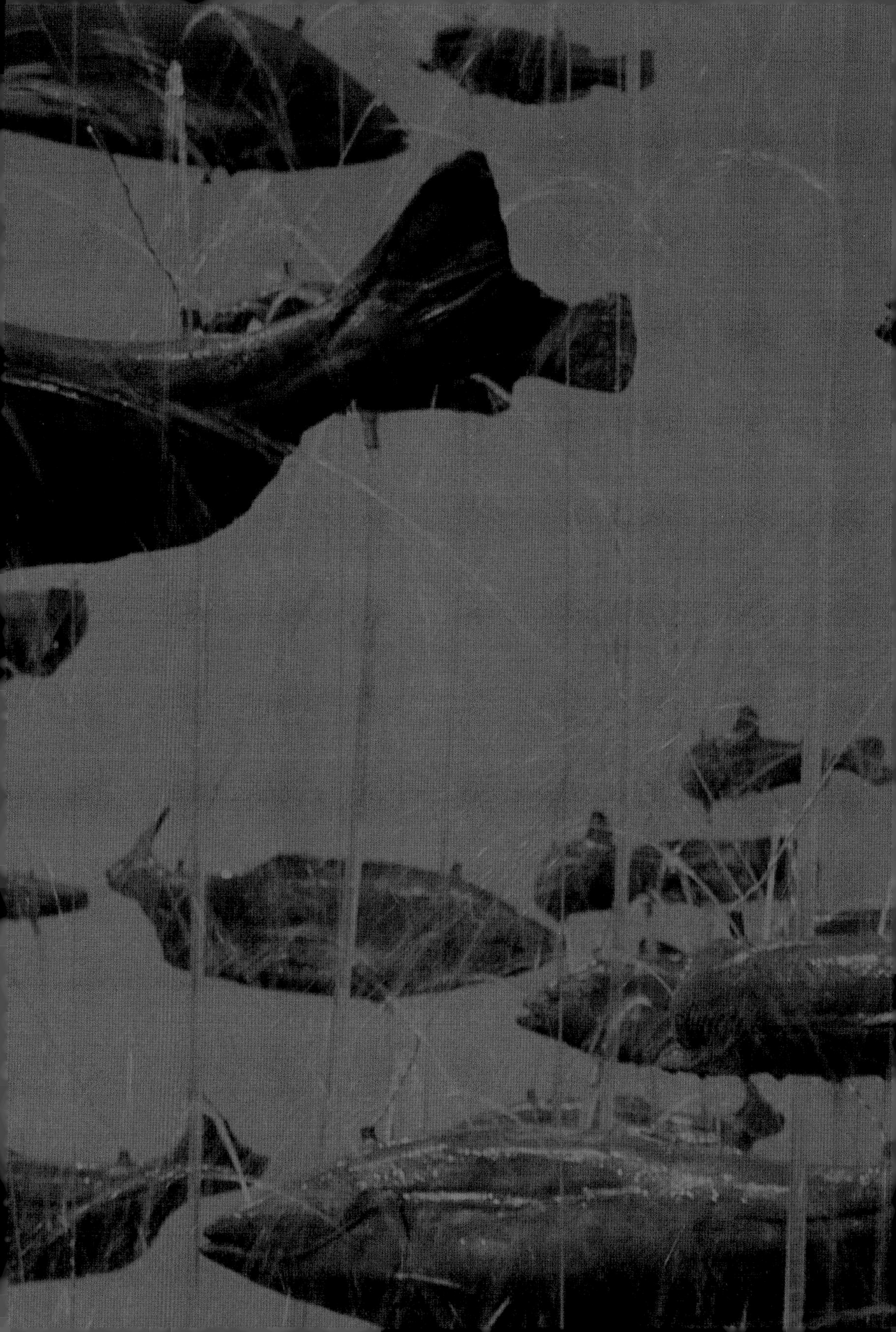

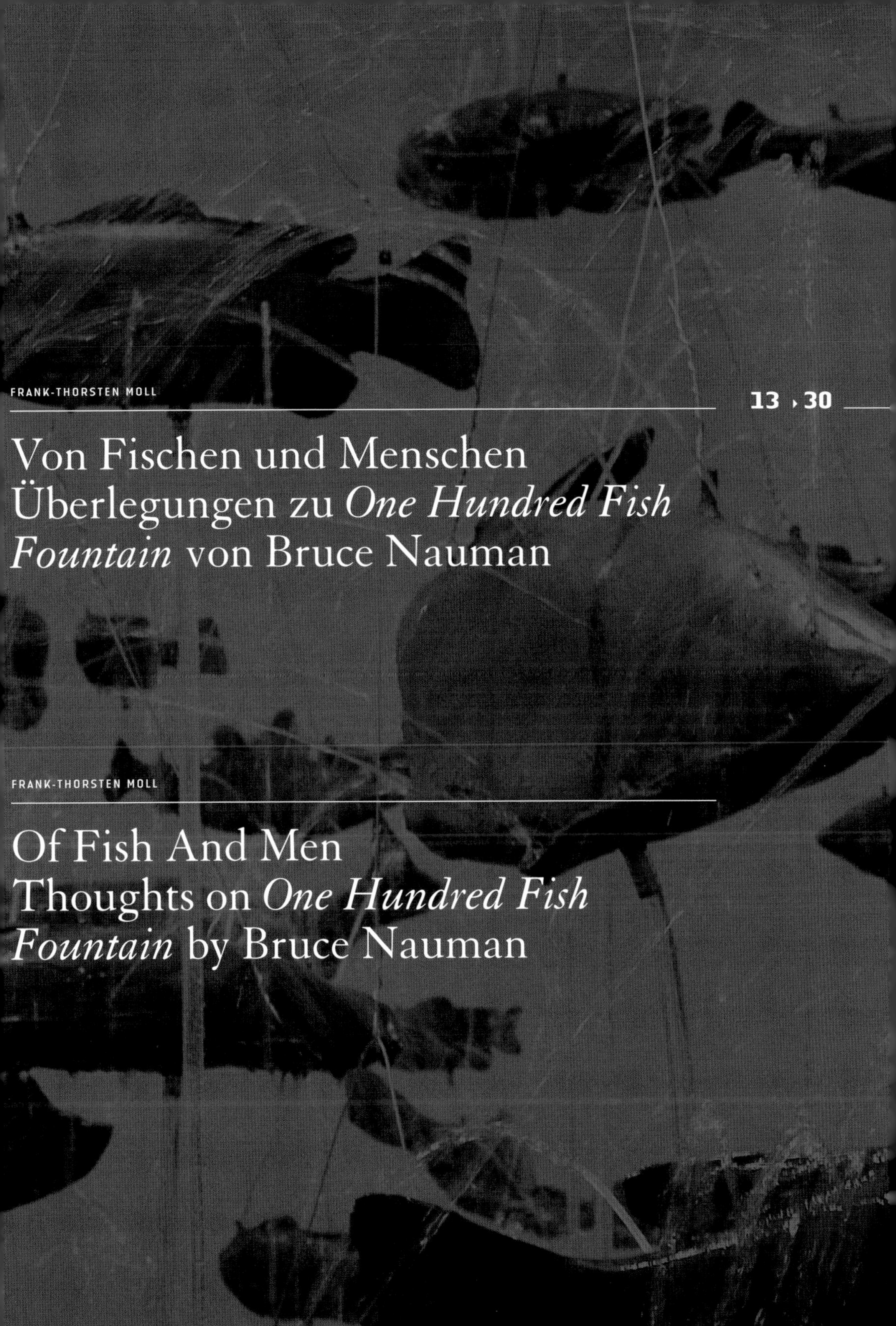

Von Fischen und Menschen
Überlegungen zu *One Hundred Fish Fountain* von Bruce Nauman

FRANK-THORSTEN MOLL

Of Fish And Men
Thoughts on *One Hundred Fish Fountain* by Bruce Nauman

»Ein ungleich anderes Erlebnis, als sich im Lehnstuhl der Malerei eines Matisse niederzulas-
sen, ist es, in Naumans Kunst Platz zu nehmen: man riskiert dabei, auf den Kopf zu fallen ...«
▶ *Robert Storr*..

Einhundert bronzene Fische hängen an Drähten von einem metallenen Gitter, durch unzählige transparente Schläuche sind sie zu einem verwirrenden Knäuel verbunden und schweben als solches über einem mit Teichfolie ausgelegten, improvisierten Bassin mitten im Ausstellungsraum. Fliegende Fische? Ein paradoxes Manöver, dass sie jedoch mit spielerischer Selbstverständlichkeit vollführen. Alles scheint auf den ersten Blick in Ordnung zu sein. Die Worte »Fische«, »Wasser« und »Brunnen« bilden zunächst einen schlüssigen Sinnzusammenhang, so als habe die Gattung des Brunnens seit hunderten von Jahren nichts anderes hervorgebracht als zu Springbrunnen arrangierte Fischschwärme. Über Pumpen am Bassinrand und ein ausgeklügeltes System von Leitungen wird den Fischen Wasser zugeführt, das sie in unterschiedlicher Intensität und Lautstärke von programmierten Intervallen gesteuert wieder ausspucken. Es entsteht ein säuselnder Geräuschteppich. Ausspeien und Einsaugen wechseln sich in so unabänderlicher Konsequenz

»Taking a seat in Nauman's art is a totally different experience than settling into the reclining
chair of the paintings by someone like Matisse; you run the risk of falling on your face ...«
▶ *Robert Storr*..

One hundred bronze fish hang on wires from a metal grid; innumerable transparent hoses join them into a confusing tangle, which hovers above an improvised basin made of plastic pond lining and placed in the middle of the exhibition space. Flying fish? A paradoxical maneuver which they execute, however, as a playful matter of course. At first glance, everything seems to be okay. The words »fish,« »water« and »fountain« at first establish a conclusive significatory coherence, as if the genre of the fountain had for hundreds of years done nothing other than to generate shoals of fish arranged into a perpetual play of water. By means of pumps along the edge of the basin and an elaborate system of hoses, the fish are filled with water, which they spew back out, with varying intensity and volume, at programmed intervals. There spreads out a carpet of murmuring sounds. The spewing out and sucking in alternate with the same irreversible consistency as the breathing in and out of the viewer and impart a precise, fundamental

ab wie das Ein- und Ausatmen des Betrachters und geben der ganzen Installation einen präzisen Rhythmus vor. Der technische Apparat, der diese Effekte produziert, bestehend aus Pumpen, Generatoren und Schläuchen, bleibt – wie es Naumans Art ist – stets sichtbar, nichts wird versteckt, kaschiert oder geschönt. Um das Schöne in seiner klassischen ästhetischen Dimension geht es Nauman ohnehin nicht im Geringsten. Auch wenn die Fische im Bronzegussverfahren naturgetreu abgeformt sind, haftet ihnen dennoch nichts Schönes, sondern viel eher etwas Groteskes an. Dicke pausbackige Fische schweben plump und ungelenk über sportlich-schlanken Vertretern ihrer Art. In ihrer Erscheinung als Gruppe haben sie durchaus etwas von einer Karikatur[01] – eines Klassentreffens vielleicht, oder ähnlichem. Es handelt sich tatsächlich um eine Art Gruppenbild, denn in dieser Installation sind die sieben gängigsten Süßwasserfischarten Nordamerikas dargestellt, allesamt Arten, die Bruce Nauman in seiner Kindheit während langer Angelausflüge mit seinem Vater selbst gefangen hat. Dadurch schwebt verhalten der Hauch eines biographischen Verweises durch die Arbeit, was einem Maß der Selbstentblößung gleichkommt, das Nauman normalerweise nicht zulassen würde. »Menschen sterben an Selbstent-

pulse to the entire installation. The technical apparatus that produces this effect consists of pumps, generators and hoses, and it remains – as is Nauman's manner – always visible; nothing is hidden, covered or touched up. Nauman is not concerned in the slightest with beauty in its classical, aesthetic dimension. Even if the fish have been so cast in bronze as to look lifelike, they in no way have a beautiful, but rather a grotesque appearance. Thick, chubby-cheeked fish hover, plump and awkward, above slender and athletic representatives of their species. In their group appearance they certainly have something of the nature of a caricature[01] – perhaps of a class reunion, or something similar. It is in fact the case of a group picture, for in this installation the seven most common types of freshwater fish in North America are represented, all species which, in his childhood, Bruce Nauman himself caught during extended fishing trips with his father. Thus the whiff of a biographical reference wafts through the work, which is tantamount to a measure of self-revelation that Nauman would normally not allow. »People die through self-revelation«[02] is the sentence in a work by Bruce Nauman, which succinctly utters the name of his most bitter antagonist ....

blößung«[02] ist der Satz in einer Arbeit, der den Namen seines ärgsten Widersachers auf den Punkt bringt. Doch wie gelingt es Nauman, diese Selbstentblößung zurückzudrängen und dem Werk selbst den Raum zu geben, der ihm gebührt? Nauman hat darauf im Lauf seiner Karriere unterschiedliche Antworten gefunden, die ich im Folgenden mit den Begriffen Leerräume, Ausschluss, Geräusche und Übergänge sortieren und in ein Fazit überführen möchte...

LEERRÄUME Die Fische sind – entgegen der Angabe im Titel – nur 97 an der Zahl und geben dadurch allein schon genug Anlass zur Verunsicherung. In der Frage nach dem Sinn ihres Fehlens schaffen die abwesenden Fische nicht nur eine unauflösbare Irritation, sondern eine Fehlstelle im Sinne eines Leerraums, der letztlich nur vom Geist des Künstlers gefüllt werden kann.[03] Das unlösbare Rätsel gibt dem Künstler eine Autorität zurück, die ihm die Kunstkritik entwendet zu haben schien. Der leere Raum, den die Fische hinterließen, als für sie entschieden wurde, für das Funktionieren der Arbeit überflüssig zu sein, ist also letztlich eine Metapher für den abwesenden Künstler selbst...
Die älteste Arbeit, die mit der Leerstelle als produktivem Faktor arbeitet, stammt aus dem Jahr 1968.

But how does Nauman manage to repel this self-revelation and impart to the work itself the space which it deserves? Over the course of his career, Nauman has responded to this question with various answers, which, in the following sections of this essay, I would like to classify with the terms empty spaces, exclusion, noises and transitions, and then proceed to a conclusion...

EMPTY SPACES The fish are – contrary to the claim made by the title – only ninety-seven in number, and thereby they already give cause enough for disquiet. In the question as to the meaning of their absence, the missing fish create not only an insoluble irritation but also an imperfection in the sense of a void, which ultimately can only be filled by the mind of the artist.[03] The unsolvable puzzle returns to the artist an authority which art criticism seems to have stolen from him. The empty space which the fish left behind, when it was decided for them that they were superfluous to the functioning of the work, is ultimately a metaphor for the absent artist himself..
The oldest work to utilize the blank space as a productive factor dates from 1968. Nauman wrote at that time the line »get out of this room, get out of my mind« on a chalkboard and hung it at the entrance to an

Nauman schrieb damals die Zeile »get out of this room, get out of my mind« auf eine Tafel und hängte sie an den Eingang eines leeren Ausstellungsraumes. Der somit ausdrücklich zurückgewiesene Besucher erlebte, insofern er die erste Abweisung ignorierte, nichts als die Tonbandstimme Naumans, die denselben Satz ständig, wenngleich mit unterschiedlicher Betonung, wiederholte. Nauman selbst beschrieb die Arbeit als Angst einflößend und viele Besucher meinten gar die Stimme Naumans aus dem Inneren ihres Kopfes als eigene vernommen zu haben. Die unerfüllt gebliebenen Seherwartungen und das Gefühl der Unerwünschtheit führten also letztlich zur vollkommenen Übereinstimmung von Künstler, Werk und Betrachter, in dessen Kopf sich der Künstler raffiniert eingenistet hatte. Der Raum war letztlich nur vom Geist des Künstlers gefüllt[04] und somit ein nicht zu lösendes Rätsel – ein Rätsel über dessen Spielregeln Bruce Nauman keine Auskunft gibt und so hängen die 97 Fische ohne ihre drei Fischkollegen herum und müssen genauso wie der Besucher mit einer frustrierenden Unvollständigkeit leben...................................
Liest man die Interviews, die Nauman in den letzten Jahren gegeben hat, so wiederholt sich darin regelmäßig die Auskunft, dass ihn letztenendes erst die Sprachlosigkeit und die Frustration ins Atelier treibt.

empty exhibition room. The visitor who was thereby turned back experienced, insofar as he ignored the first dismissal, nothing except for Nauman's recorded voice repeating the same sentence again and again, albeit with varying intonation. Nauman himself described the work as instilling fear, and many visitors believed themselves to have heard Nauman's voice from inside their own heads as their personal voices. The unfulfilled expectation of seeing something and the feeling of being unwanted ultimately led to a perfect harmony between the artist, his work and the viewer, in whose head the artist had cleverly inserted himself. The space was ultimately filled only with the spirit of the artist[04] and thus existed as an insoluble conundrum – a puzzle about whose rules Bruce Nauman gave no information; similarly, the ninety-seven fish dangling in midair remain deprived of their piscine colleagues and are required, just like the visitor, to live with a frustrating incompleteness..
If one reads the interviews, which Nauman has given in recent years, there is a regular repetition of the information that it is ultimately speechlessness and frustration that drive him into the studio. Thus it is not really surprising that the viewer finds frustration to constitute the most productive access to Nauman's work........

Deshalb verwundert es nicht wirklich, wenn der Betrachter über die Frustration den wohl produktivsten Zugang zu Naumans Werk findet ....

AUSGRENZUNG In den frühen Arbeiten der 1960er Jahre hatte sich eine bewusste Betonung der Mitte des jeweiligen Ausstellungsraumes im Werk Bruce Naumans bereits angekündigt. Die per Video festgehaltenen Atelierbegehungen können als Beispiel für diese Tendenz herhalten. Durch die Stuhl- und Tierkarussells, die Nauman im Anschluss daran fertigte, wird zunächst die Peripherie und nicht der Mittelpunkt artikuliert und die Bewegungsfreiheit des Betrachters zunehmend eingeschränkt. Der Schritt ins Zentrum bleibt ihm zumeist verwehrt. Die Bewegungsfähigkeit ist eingeschränkt und so wird die Mitte des Raumes selbst schon zur Leerstelle, die dem Raum seine Ordnung diktiert und in der Ökonomie der Inszenierung die dominierende Rolle einnimmt. Dem Besucher bleibt nur übrig, sich zu der Installation dahingehend zu verhalten, dass er ihren Platz in der Mitte akzeptiert und sie vorsichtig umkreist.[05] Grundsätzlich fällt auf, dass Nauman den Aspekt der Bewegung mehr und mehr auf den Betrachter verlagert – seine Tierskulpturen sind nicht mehr wie zu Beginn motorbetriebene Karussells, sondern statische Mobiles – was

EXCLUSION In the early works from the nineteen-sixties, a deliberate emphasis on the center of the respective exhibition space had already announced itself in the works of Bruce Nauman. The studio visits recorded on video could serve as an example of this tendency. Through the chair- and animal-carousels which Nauman subsequently produced, first the periphery and not the center is articulated, so that the viewer's freedom to move is increasingly restricted. Most of the time he was denied the step into the center. Freedom of movement is restricted, and thus the middle of the space itself already becomes a void that dictates its order to the space and assumes the dominating role in the economy of the staging. The visitor only has the possibility of responding to the installation by accepting its place in the middle and cautiously moving around it.[05] What is most striking is the fact that Nauman shifts the aspect of movement more and more onto the viewer – his animal sculptures are no longer motor-driven carousels, as at the beginning, but are instead static mobiles – which already represents a paradox in itself. The sculpture can achieve its dominance all the more, inasmuch as its playful aspect is greatly attenuated. In the case of *One Hundred Fish Fountain*, the fish themselves take on a strategy of exclusion. Even though they are grouped around an

an sich schon ein Paradoxon darstellt. Ihre Dominanz kann die Skulptur dadurch umso besser entfalten, da ihr spielerischer Aspekt stark abgemildert ist. Im Fall von *One Hundred Fish Fountain* übernehmen die Fische selbst eine Strategie der Ausgrenzung. Zwar sind sie um eine imaginäre Mitte gruppiert, der größte Teil der Fische schaut jedoch mit dem wasserspeienden und deshalb geöffneten Maul Richtung Betrachter, als wollten sie die Arbeit »get out of this room, get out of my mind« gemeinsam anstimmen und damit neu aufleben lassen..
Die Strategie, dem Betrachter die Möglichkeit zu verwehren in die Mitte des Raumes zu gelangen, ist also nicht neu und hat nicht erst mit den politischen Arbeiten *South American Triangle* von 1981 ihren historischen Startpunkt. Dörte Zbikowski wies in ihrem Katalogaufsatz[06] zu Recht darauf hin, dass bereits die *cones cojones* Arbeiten der Jahre 1973 bis 1975 durch ihre Verdichtungen von geometrischen Linien und Formen dem Besucher klar machten, dass die Regie im Raum ein anderer führt – nämlich der Künstler selbst. Auch in Anbetracht des Fischbrunnens scheint dieser zu sagen »you will never get to the middle of this room, get out of my mind (you will never understand)«..

imaginary middle, a considerable majority of the fish look in the direction of the viewer with their water-spewing and accordingly open mouths, as if together they wished to intone and thereby resurrect the work »get out of this room, get out of my mind« ....
The strategy of prohibiting the viewer access to the middle of the room is not new and did not have its historical point of departure with the political works *South American Triangle* from 1981. In her catalogue essay,[06] Dörte Zbikowski correctly pointed to the fact that already the *cones cojones* works from 1973 to 1975 made it clear to the visitor, through their condensing of geometrical lines and forms, that someone else was conducting the stage direction in the space – namely the artist himself. Also in consideration of the fish fountain, the artist seemed to be saying, »You will never get to the middle of this room, get out of my mind (you will never understand)« ....
The hanging sculptures of the nineteen-eighties take over the concept of the *cones cojones*, and particularly the animal sculptures in polyurethane radiate this defensive behavior. The heads of the animal forms mostly hang such that they point outwards, away from the middle of their community or of the space in

Die Hängeskulpturen der 1980er übernehmen das Konzept der *cones cojones* und gerade die Tierskulpturen aus Polyurethan strahlen diese Abwehrhaltung aus. Die Köpfe der Tierformen hängen zumeist so, dass sie nach außen zeigen, weg von der Mitte ihrer Gemeinschaft oder des Raumes, in dem sie sich befinden. In der Serie der *musical chairs* oder der bereits zitierten Arbeit *South American Triangle* von 1981 sind es die beweglichen Stahlträger, die den Betrachter sprichwörtlich wegdrängen...
Die Erfahrung von Ausschluss ist in seinen Arbeiten jedoch nicht nur bloßer Effekt, sondern Antrieb für den Künstler selbst. »Solche Dinge, an die man nicht herankommt, erzeugen viel Wut. Das gehört zum Inhalt der Arbeit – und auch zu ihrer Entstehungsgeschichte. Wut und Enttäuschung sind Gefühle, die eine starke Antriebskraft für mich sind. Sie treiben mich ins Atelier, in die Arbeit hinein.«[07].....................
GERÄUSCH ALS MATERIAL DER SKULPTUR Geräusche und Klänge erweitern von jeher die visuelle Wahrnehmung des Werkes von Bruce Nauman. Früher, zum Beispiel bei seinen Geharbeiten, in denen er den Atelierraum mit choreographierten Schritten durchmaß, stand oftmals die banale Handlung des Künstlerindividuums im Mittelpunkt. Später, in seinen Clownarbeiten, wurde die Soundebene durch die nervtötende

which they are located. In the series of the *musical chairs*, or the aforementioned *South American Triangle* from 1981, it is the movable steel beams which proverbially repulse the viewer...
In Nauman's works, however, the experience of exclusion is not mere effect, but rather the driving impulse for the artist himself. »The sort of things that you can't get at create a lot of anger. That belongs to the contents of the work – and also to the history of its creation. Anger and disappointment are feelings that are a strong driving force for me. They propel me into the studio, into the work.«[07].....................................
NOISE AS A MATERIAL OF SCULPTURE Noise and sounds have from the very beginning complemented the visual perception of the works of Bruce Nauman. Earlier, for example with his performance pieces in which he measured out the studio space in choreographed steps, it was often the banal actions of the artistic individual which was focused upon. Later, with his clown works, the acoustic level became increasingly important with the enervating repetition and variation of words and sentences that were always the same. The filmed protagonist thus kept a grip on everything. The strands of the artistic narration coalesced in him. At the same time that Bruce Nauman withdrew more and more from the public life of a recognized

Wiederholung und Variation der immer gleichen Sätze und Wörter zunehmend wichtiger. Der gefilmte Akteur behielt dabei die Fäden in der Hand. In ihm liefen die Stränge der künstlerischen Narration zusammen. Zur selben Zeit, als sich Bruce Nauman mehr und mehr aus dem öffentlichen Leben eines anerkannten Künstlers in die Privatheit seiner Farm im Norden von New Mexiko zurückzog, übertrug er die Rolle des Akteurs auf tierische Agenten – in diesem Fall auf 97 Fische. Wiederholung und Endlosloops übernehmen sie bereitwillig durch die »rituelle Litanei«[08] des geräuschvollen Wasserspiels.......................
Der Künstler leitet von diesen Klangebenen nicht nur eine Erweiterung seines Skulpturbegriffs ab, sondern ist sich durchaus darüber im Klaren, dass mit ihnen eine Belästigung des Betrachters einhergeht. Über seine Neonarbeiten, zu deren visueller Erscheinung die Transformatoren einen gehörigen Geräuschpegel beisteuerten, sagte er einmal folgendes: »Manchmal fühlten sich die Leute von diesen Geräuschen gestört. Sie hätten die Arbeiten lieber vollkommen still gehabt. Klänge und Geräusche haben etwas Unmittelbares, Aufdringliches an sich, dem man nicht aus dem Weg gehen kann.«[09] Er machte dadurch klar, dass Geräusche, ähnlich effektiv wie die Besetzung der Mitte des Raumes, durch die physische Präsenz der

artist into the privacy of his ranch in Northern New Mexico, he transferred the role of the protagonist onto animal agents – in the present case onto ninety-seven fishes. They readily take on repetitions and endless loops through the »ritualized litany«[08] of the noisy fountain..
From these levels of sound, the artist not only derives an expansion of his concept of sculpture but is also quite aware of the fact that along with them comes the imposition of a burden onto the viewer. Concerning his neon works, to whose visual appearance the transformers add a pertinent noise level, he has the following to say: »Sometimes people are disturbed by these noises. They would have preferred for the works to be utterly still. Sounds and noises have something direct and insistent about them that you can't just avoid.«[09] He thereby made it clear that noises function in a similarly effective manner as the occupying of the middle of the room by the physical presence of the sculpture. In 2004 Nauman showed how important the acoustic dimension and the control of the space through sound were to him when he took on a difficult challenge, namely the staging of a spectacle in the Turbine Hall of the Tate Modern in London. This hall, which Martin Gayfordan describes as »the secret headquarters of the villain in a James Bond film,«[10]

Skulptur funktionieren. Wie wichtig ihm die akustische Dimension und die Kontrolle des Raums durch Sound ist, zeigte Nauman 2004, als er sich einer harten Aufgabe stellte: der Bespielung der Turbinenhalle der Tate Modern in London. Die Halle, die Martin Gayford an »das geheime Hauptquartier eines Bösewichts aus einem James Bond Film«[10] erinnert, warf Schwierigkeiten auf, denen Nauman mit der Arbeit *raw materials* perfekt zu begegnen wusste. Auf die Dominanz des Raumes antwortete er mit einer Art Anthologie seiner alten Video-/Sound-/Textarbeiten, deren Aufnahmen aus insegesamt 35 von Lautsprechern auf den Besucher niederprasselten – womit er ein an den Turmbau von Babel erinnerndes Gemisch an Stimmen entfesselte. Dies habe – so Gayford – die Arbeit mehr zu einer Skulptur werden lassen, als zu einem Drama oder einem Musikstück. Die Arbeit führt den Betrachter im Raum herum, zwingt ihn zu Entscheidungen über Standortwahl und Verweildauer und ist anders als eine Performance die ganze Zeit »anwesend«. Andererseits ist sie aber auch nie dieselbe, eben nur beinahe.[11] Erneut erinnert seine Strategie an die eines wild gewordenen Komponisten, der seine Stücke parallel zur Aufführung bringt. Nauman, der neben seinem Studium der Mathematik, Physik und Kunst auch Bass in einer Jazzband spielte, zeigt in der

presented difficulties that Nauman knew how to surmount perfectly with the work *Raw Materials*. He responded to the dominance of the space with a sort of anthology of his old video/sound/text works, whose recordings rained down upon the visitor from exactly 35 loudspeakers – whereby he unleashed a cacophony of voices recalling the Tower of Babel. According to Gayfordan, this transformed the work into more of a sculpture than a drama or a musical piece. The work guides the viewer around the space, compels him to decisions with regard to where and how long to remain at one place and is, in contrast to a performance, »present« for the entire time. On the other hand, it is never the same, only almost so.[11] Once again, his strategy recalls that of a composer who has grown wild and who wishes for his pieces to be performed in parallel. Nauman, who alongside his studies of mathematics, physics and art also played bass guitar in a jazz band, shows in the statements concerning his personal heroes and models how important music has remained to him. His heroes are as a rule not artists and seldom literary figures such as, for example, Samuel Beckett, but most often musicians such as John Coltrane and Lenny Tristano, who has in the meantime been forgotten. When he was asked why he thinks about the latter so much and what he had

Auskunft über seine persönlichen Helden und Vorbilder, wie wichtig ihm die Musik bis heute geblieben ist. Seine Helden sind in der Regel keine Künstler und nur selten Literaten wie z.B. Samuel Beckett, sondern zumeist Musiker wie John Coltrane und der mittlerweile vergessene Lenny Tristano. Als er gefragt wurde, warum er so viel an ihn denke und was er von ihm habe lernen können, sagte er: »Wenn Lenny gut spielte, hat es einen voll erwischt – bis zur letzten Note. Er hörte dann einfach abrupt auf zu spielen. Man bekam bei ihm keine Einleitung, keinen Ausklang – nur volle Intensität, zwei oder zwanzig Minuten lang, als würde man aus einem Coltrane-Stück die Mitte herausnehmen – den härtesten, schwierigsten Teil. Das war alles. Ich habe von Anfang an versucht, Kunst zu machen, die so auf die Menschen einwirkte, die sofort voll da war. Wie ein Hieb ins Gesicht mit dem Baseballschläger, oder besser, wie ein Schlag ins Genick. Man sieht den Schlag nicht kommen, er haut einen einfach um. Die Idee gefällt mir sehr, diese Art von Intensität, die einem keinen Anhaltspunkt gibt, herauszufinden, ob man die Arbeit mag oder nicht.«[12]........

FLIESSENDE ÜBERGÄNGE In einer seiner ersten filmischen Arbeiten mit dem Titel *Fishing for Asian Carp* (1966) sieht man einen Mann, der seine Anglerstiefel anzieht, in einen Fluss steigt und schließlich einen Fisch

been able to learn from him, Nauman replied, »When Lenny played well, he grabbed you down deep – right to the very last note. Then he simply stopped playing. You didn't get an introduction with him, no fading away – only full intensity for two or twenty minutes, as if you were to take the middle section out of a Coltrane piece – the hardest, most difficult part. That was all. From the very beginning I tried to create art that had this sort of effect on people, that was fully present right from the start. Like a smash in the face with a baseball bat, or better, like a blow to the neck. You don't see it coming, it just knocks you down. I like that idea a lot, this sort of intensity that doesn't give you grounds for finding out whether you like the work or not.«[12] ....

FLOWING TRANSITIONS In one of Nauman's first film works with the title *Fishing for Asian Carp* (1966), one sees a man putting on his fishing boots, stepping into a river and then catching a fish. The film is exactly as long as it takes to catch the fish: two minutes and forty-four seconds. The film as it stands is thus the product of pure chance, a game with uncertain outcome – for what would happen if the man had simply failed to catch any fish before the film was over? *Fishing for Asian Carp* is doubtlessly also an allegory of the unpredictability

fängt. Der Film ist gerade so lang, wie es dauert, bis der Fisch gefangen ist: 2 Minuten und 44 Sekunden. Der entstehende Film ist also Produkt reinen Zufalls, ein Spiel mit ungewissem Ausgang – denn was wäre, wenn der Mann einfach keinen Fisch gefangen hätte, bevor die Filmspule abgelaufen war? Zweifellos ist also *Fishing for Asian Carp* auch eine Allegorie auf die Unvorhersehbarkeit des künstlerischen Prozesses – das gelungene Werk wird halb ironisch, halb ernsthaft (wie so häufig bei den frühen Arbeiten Naumans) in Eins gesetzt mit dem glücklichen Fang des Anglers. Picassos berühmter Ausspruch »Ich suche nicht, ich finde« erfährt hier eine eigenwillige Neuinterpretation. Diese Arbeit wie auch *Self-Portrait as a Fountain* (1966/67) könnten sich durch ihren performativen Charakter nicht widersprüchlicher zu *One Hundred Fish Fountain* verhalten. Doch es zeigt sich in diesen Arbeiten prototypisch das grundsätzliche Interesse von Nauman, das schon früh an den »fließenden Übergängen zwischen Performance und Installation, zwischen Aufführung und Ausstellung«[13] festzumachen war. Diese Beobachtung Beltings ist sicher zutreffend, denn bei kaum einem zeitgenössischen Künstler fällt die Kategorisierung so schwer wie bei Nauman. In den 1960ern beschäftigte sich Nauman mit der Wahrnehmung des Betrachters im Raum der

of the artistic process: The successfully achieved work is, in a half ironic, half serious manner (as so often with Nauman's early works), presented as equivalent to the fortunate catch of the fisherman. Picasso's famous statement »I don't seek, I find« here experiences a idiosyncratic reinterpretation. This work, just like *Self Portrait as a Fountain* (1966/67), could not in its performative character stand in more pronounced opposition to *One Hundred Fish Fountain*. But these works prototypically express Nauman's fundamental interest that could be discerned early on with regard to the »flowing transitions between performance and installation, between staging and exhibition.«[13] This observation by Belting is certainly apposite, for with scarcely another contemporary artist does categorization prove to be so difficult as with Nauman. In the nineteen-sixties, he focused his attention on the visitor's perception in the space of the gallery or museum; he accordingly captured the viewer in a closed-circuit process and caused him to wander through narrow corridors. The result of this practice, according to Belting, is a divided experience of the work which may only be conveyed in contradictory descriptions. On the one hand, the viewer experiences a highly subjective situation which he summons up in remembrance through vivid impressions – but on the other, these cannot

Galerie oder des Museums, er fing ihn deshalb im Verfahren des »closed circuit« ein und ließ den Betrachter in engen Korridoren umherirren. Resultat dieser Praxis, so Belting, ist eine zweigeteilte Werkerfahrung, die sich nur in widersprüchlichen Beschreibungen fassen lasse. Der Betrachter erlebt zum einen eine höchst subjektive Situation, die er sich über starke Eindrücke in Erinnerung ruft – diese können jedoch durch keine Reproduktion ersetzt werden. Das Werk funktioniert also nur in der Summe aller gesammelter Eindrücke. Dabei passiert etwas Unerwartetes: »Das alte Werkoriginal kehrt ausgerechnet dort, wo man es nicht mehr auf den Begriff bringen kann, in einem originalen Werkeindruck wieder, der sich zu verselbständigen scheint. Der Eindruck in einer Installation lebt von der Aura des ›Hier und Jetzt‹ (Walter Benjamin), die doch einmal die klassische Werkerfahrung ausgemacht hat.«[14] Für Belting ist dies ein untrügliches Zeichen dafür, dass unter der bekannten Oberfläche des Werks eine weitere Ebene aufscheint, die anthropologische Fragestellungen ahnen lässt ....

VOM MENSCHEN Für Nauman sind die Tierskulpturen, zu denen *One Hundred Fish Fountain* zweifellos gezählt werden muss, immer auch ein Verweis auf den Menschen selbst, indem sie in gewisser Weise einen

be replaced by any reproduction whatsoever. Hence the work functions only in the sum of all gathered impressions, whereupon something unexpected occurs. »The old original of the work returns, there where it is no longer possible to equate it with a concept, into an original impression of the work. The impression in an installation lives from the aura of the ›here and now‹ (Walter Benjamin) which once constituted the classical experience of a work.«[14] For Belting this is an unmistakable sign that, beneath the familiar surface of a work, there shines forth a further level that hints at anthropological issues......................................

OF HUMAN BEINGS For Nauman the animal sculptures, among which *One Hundred Fish Fountain* must certainly be numbered, also always refer to the human being himself, inasmuch as in a certain manner they represent a particular myth of society. The investigation of the social and systemic bondage of the subject also stands at the hidden center of his oeuvre and leaves clearly discernable traces which run though all of his creative phases. The animal works, which also in the evaluation of Dorothée Brill reveal the bondage of human beings to patterns of social behavior,[15] are almost always detached, however, from a concrete political component. The late works thus stand in opposition to his early steel mobiles as political commentaries,

bestimmten Mythos von Gesellschaft repräsentieren. Die Befragung der sozialen und systemischen Gebundenheit des Subjektes steht auch im verborgenen Zentrum seines Werks und legt eine deutlich sichtbare Spur aus, die sich durch alle Schaffensperioden hindurchzieht. Die Tierarbeiten, die auch in der Einschätzung Dorothée Brills die Gebundenheit des Menschen an gesellschaftliche Verhaltensmuster offenbaren[15], sind allerdings fast immer losgelöst von einer konkret politischen Komponente. Die späten Arbeiten stehen somit im Gegensatz zu seinen als politische Kommentare zu verstehende frühen Stahlmobiles, die Ausdruck der Enttäuschung über die conditio humana am Beispiel der Menschenrechtsverletzungen in einigen Staaten Lateinamerikas waren. Auslöser für die künstlerische Arbeit ist für Nauman immer die rohe

which were an expression of disappointment about the human condition with reference to human rights violations in several countries of Latin America. For Nauman, the catalyst for artistic work is always the raw energy of frustration and speechlessness. »At some point I simply get started with making something, regardless of whether it's with a good idea, a bad idea or no idea. I just make something out of what is lying around. And precisely these things that arise out of speechlessness, out of despair, are often the most

Energie von Frustration und Sprachlosigkeit. »Irgendwann fange ich dann einfach an, irgendwas zu machen, ganz egal ob mit guter Idee, schlechter Idee, keiner Idee. Ich mache einfach etwas aus dem, was so herumliegt. Und gerade diese Dinge, die aus einer Sprachlosigkeit heraus entstehen, aus Verzweiflung heraus, sind oft die wichtigsten. Sie führen zum Kern, zu der Frage, wer ich bin und warum ich überhaupt irgendetwas tun will.«[16] ....

Bestimmt liegt gerade in Naumans stetem Ringen um die schiere Möglichkeit, Kunst in Anbetracht aller Hemmnisse und Unwägbarkeit konstant neu zu denken, seine wahre Größe, die ihn zum Vorbild für Generationen jüngerer Künstler und zum Gegenstand hymnischer Besprechungen gemacht hat ....

important ones. They lead to the core, to the question as to who I am and why I want to do anything at all.«[16] ....

It is doubtlessly in Nauman's tireless wrestling with the sheer possibility of constantly conceiving art anew, in view of all hindrances and imponderabilities, that there lies the true greatness which has made him a model for generations of younger artists and the subject of hymnlike discussions...

▶ 01 DIE TENDENZ ZUM KARIKATURHAFTEN KOMMT IN FOLGENDEM ZITAT ZUM AUSDRUCK: »ÜBER MEHRERE JAHRE HINWEG HATTE NAUMAN DER MENSCHLICHEN FIGUR IN DER KARIKIEREND-GEWALTTÄTIGEN ÜBERZEICHNUNG VON NEONOBJEKT ODER CLOWNSMASKERADE GESTALT GEGEBEN.« ZIT. NACH DOROTHÉE BRILL: *Animal Sculptures*. IN: GÖTZ ADRIANI (HRSG.): *Bruce Nauman. Werke aus der Sammlung Froehlich und FER*. MUSEUM FÜR NEUE KUNST, ZKM KARLSRUHE, OSTFILDERN-RUIT 1999, S. 139–148. HIER: S. 144 ▶ 02 ZIT. NACH HANNO RAUTERBERG: *Die Kunst erlöst uns von gar nichts. Im Gespräch mit Bruce Nauman*. IN: DIE ZEIT, VOM 14.10.2004 ▶ 03 ZIT. NACH DÖRTE ZBIKOWSKI: *Betrachter und Rezipienten*. IN: GÖTZ ADRIANI (HRSG.), *Bruce Nauman, Werke aus der Sammlung Froehlich und FER*, MUSEUM FÜR NEUE KUNST, ZKM KARLSRUHE, OSTFILDERN-RUIT, 1999, S. 9–27. HIER: S. 17 ▶ 04 EBENDA, S.17 ▶ 05 VGL. JÖRG ZUTTER (HRSG.): *Bruce Nauman. Skulpturen und Installationen 1985–1990*. KÖLN 1991. S. 45 FF ▶ 06 ZIT. NACH DÖRTE ZBIKOWSKI: *Betrachter und Rezipienten*. IN: GÖTZ ADRIANI (HRSG.): *Bruce Nauman. Werke aus der Sammlung Froehlich und FER*. MUSEUM FÜR NEUE KUNST, ZKM KARLSRUHE, OSTFILDERN-RUIT 1999, S. 9–27 ▶ 07 ZIT. NACH *Das Schweigen brechen. Ein Interview mit Joan Simon*. IN: *Bruce Nauman. Interviews 1967–1988*. AUS DEM AMERIKANISCHEN UND HERAUSGEGEBEN VON CHRISTINE HOFFMANN, DRESDEN 1996, S. 147–177. HIER: S. 169 ▶ 08 ZIT. NACH DÖRTE ZBIKOWSKI: *Betrachter und Rezipienten*.

▶ 01 THE TENDENCY TOWARDS CARICATURE FINDS EXPRESSION IN THE FOLLOWING QUOTATION: »FOR A PERIOD OF SEVERAL YEARS, NAUMAN HAD SHAPED THE HUMAN FIGURE IN THE CARICATURAL-VIOLENT EXAGGERATION OF NEON OBJECT OR CLOWN MASQUERADE.« QUOTE FROM DOROTHÉE BRILL: *Animal Sculptures*. IN: GÖTZ ADRIANI (ED.): *Bruce Nauman. Werke aus der Sammlung Froehlich und FER* (BRUCE NAUMAN. WORKS FROM THE FROEHLICH AND FER COLLECTION). MUSEUM FÜR NEUE KUNST, ZKM KARLSRUHE, OSTFILDERN-RUIT 1999, PP. 139–148. HERE: P. 144 ▶ 02 QUOTED FROM HANNO RAUTERBERG: *Die Kunst erlöst uns von gar nichts* (ART DOESN'T FREE US FROM ANYTHING). IN A CONVERSATION WITH BRUCE NAUMAN. IN: DIE ZEIT, 10.14.2004 ▶ 03 QUOTED FROM DÖRTE ZBIKOWSKI: *Betrachter und Rezipienten* (VIEWER AND RECIPIENT). IN: GÖTZ ADRIANI (ED.): *Bruce Nauman. Werke aus der Sammlung Froehlich und FER*. MUSEUM FÜR NEUE KUNST, ZKM KARLSRUHE, OSTFILDERN-RUIT 1999, PP. 9–27. HERE: P. 17 ▶ 04 IBID., P. 17 ▶ 05 CF. JÖRG ZUTTER (ED.): *Bruce Nauman. Skulpturen und Installationen 1985–1990* (BRUCE NAUMAN, SCULPTURES AND INSTALLATIONS 1985–1990). COLOGNE 1991, P. 45 FF ▶ 06 QUOTED FROM DÖRTE ZBIKOWSKI: *Betrachter und Rezipienten* (VIEWER AND RECIPIENT). IN: GÖTZ ADRIANI (ED.): *Bruce Nauman. Werke aus der Sammlung Froehlich und FER*. MUSEUM FÜR NEUE KUNST, ZKM KARLSRUHE, OSTFILDERN-RUIT 1999, PP. 9–27 ▶ 07 QUOTED FROM *Das Schweigen Brechen, Ein Interview mit Joan Simon* (BREAKING THE SILENCE, AN INTERVIEW WITH JOAN SIMON). IN: *Bruce Nauman. Interviews 1967–1988*. TRANSLATED AND EDITED BY CHRISTINE HOFFMANN, DRESDEN 1996, PP. 147–177. HERE: P. 169 ▶ 08 QUOTED FROM DÖRTE ZBIKOWSKI: *Betrachter und Rezipienten* (VIEWER

In: Götz Adriani (Hrsg.): *Bruce Nauman. Werke aus der Sammlung Froehlich und FER.* Museum für Neue Kunst, ZKM Karlsruhe, Ostfildern-Ruit 1999, S. 9–27. Hier: S.18 ▶ **09** Zit. nach *Das Schweigen brechen. Ein Interview mit Joan Simon.* In: *Bruce Nauman. Interviews 1967–1988.* Aus dem Amerikanischen und herausgegeben von Christine Hoffmann, Dresden 1996, S. 147–177. Hier: S. 171–172 ▶ **10** Zit. nach Martin Gayford: *Sculpture for the ears.* Interview mit Bruce Nauman anlässlich seiner Retrospektive in der Tate Modern, The Daily Telegraph vom 10.12.2004 ▶ **11** Vgl. ebenda ▶ **12** Zit. nach *Das Schweigen brechen. Ein Interview mit Joan Simon.* In: *Bruce Nauman. Interviews 1967–1988.* Aus dem Amerikanischen und herausgegeben von Christine Hoffmann, Verlag der Kunst, Dresden 1996, S. 147–177 ▶ **13** Zit. nach Hans Belting: *Das Unsichtbare Meisterwerk. Die modernen Mythen der Kunst.* München 1998, S. 451 ▶ **14** ebenda, S.465 ▶ **15** Vgl. Dorothée Brill: *Animal Sculptures.* In: Götz Adriani (Hrsg.): *Bruce Nauman. Werke aus der Sammlung Froehlich und FER.* Museum für Neue Kunst, ZKM Karlsruhe, Ostfildern-Ruit 1999, S.139–148 ▶ **16** Zit. nach Hanno Rauterberg: *Die Kunst erlöst uns von gar nichts. Im Gespräch mit Bruce Nauman.* In: DIE ZEIT, vom 14.10.2004 ....

....

and Recipient). In: Götz Adriani (ed.): *Bruce Nauman. Werke aus der Sammlung Froehlich und FER.* Museum für Neue Kunst, ZKM Karlsruhe, Ostfildern-Ruit 1999, pp. 9–27. Here p. 18 ▶ **09** Quoted from *Das Schweigen Brechen, Ein Interview mit Joan Simon* (Breaking the Silence, An Interview with Joan Simon). In: *Bruce Nauman. Interviews 1967–1988.* Translated and edited by Christine Hoffmann, Dresden 1996, pp. 147–177. Here: pp. 171–172 ▶ **10** Quoted from Martin Gayford: *Sculpture for the ears.* Interview with Bruce Nauman on the occasion of his Retrospective in the Tate Modern, The Daily Telegraph, 12.10.2004 ▶ **11** Ibid. ▶ **12** Quoted from *Das Schweigen Brechen, Ein Interview mit Joan Simon* (Breaking the Silence, An Interview with Joan Simon). In: *Bruce Nauman. Interviews 1967–1988.* Translated and edited by Christine Hoffmann, Dresden 1996, pp. 147–177 ▶ **13** Quoted from Hans Belting: *Das unsichtbare Meisterwerk. Die modernen Mythen der Kunst* (The Invisible Masterpiece, The Modern Myths of Art). Munich 1998, p. 451 ▶ **14** Ibid., p. 465 ▶ **15** Quote from Dorothée Brill: *Animal Sculptures.* In: Götz Adriani (ed.): *Bruce Nauman. Werke aus der Sammlung Froehlich und FER* (Bruce Nauman. Works from the Froehlich and FER Collection). Museum für Neue Kunst, ZKM Karlsruhe, Ostfildern-Ruit 1999, pp. 139–148 ▶ **16** Quoted from Hanno Rauterberg: *Die Kunst erlöst uns von gar nichts* (Art doesn't free us from anything). In a conversation with Bruce Nauman. In: DIE ZEIT, 10.14.2004 ....

....

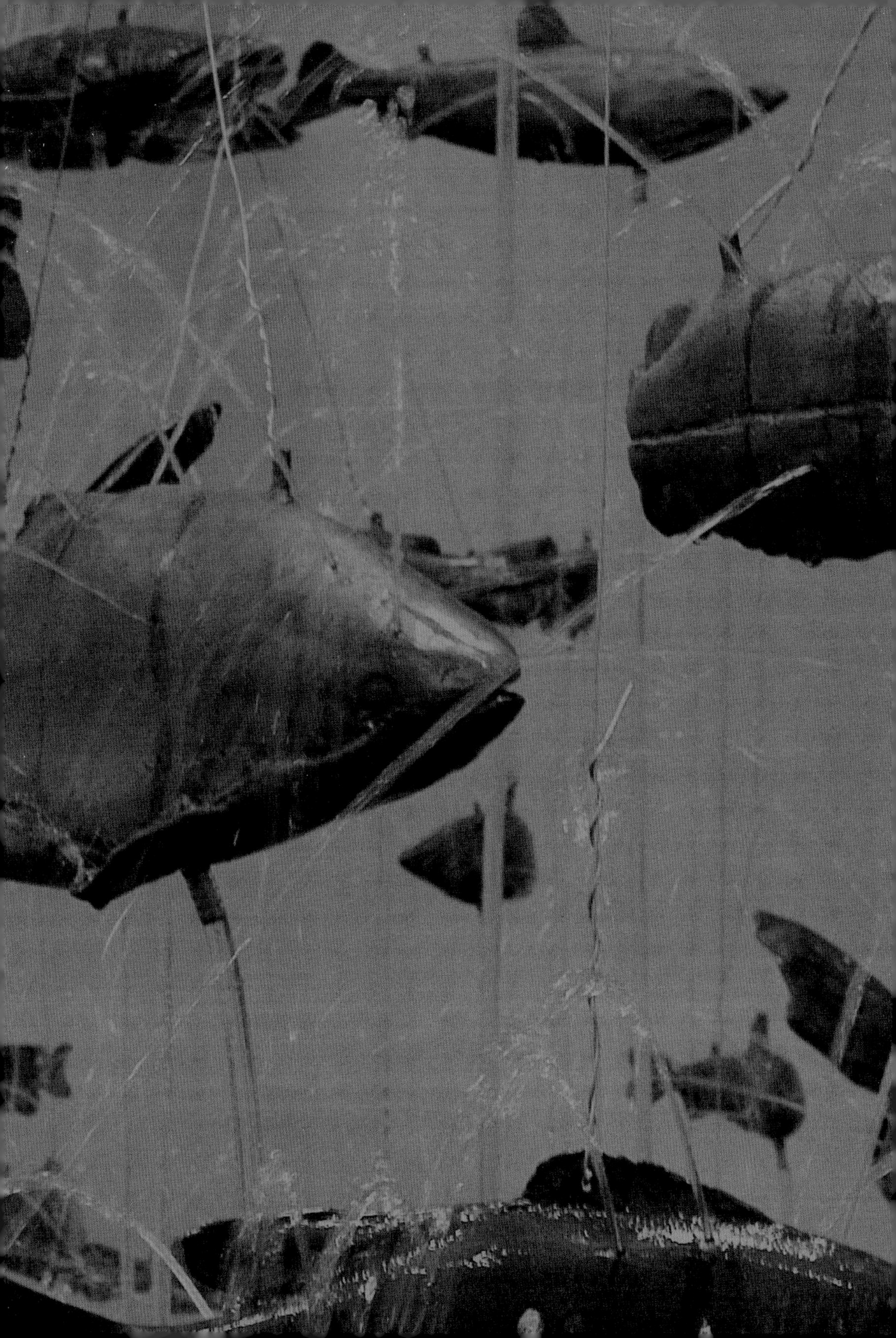

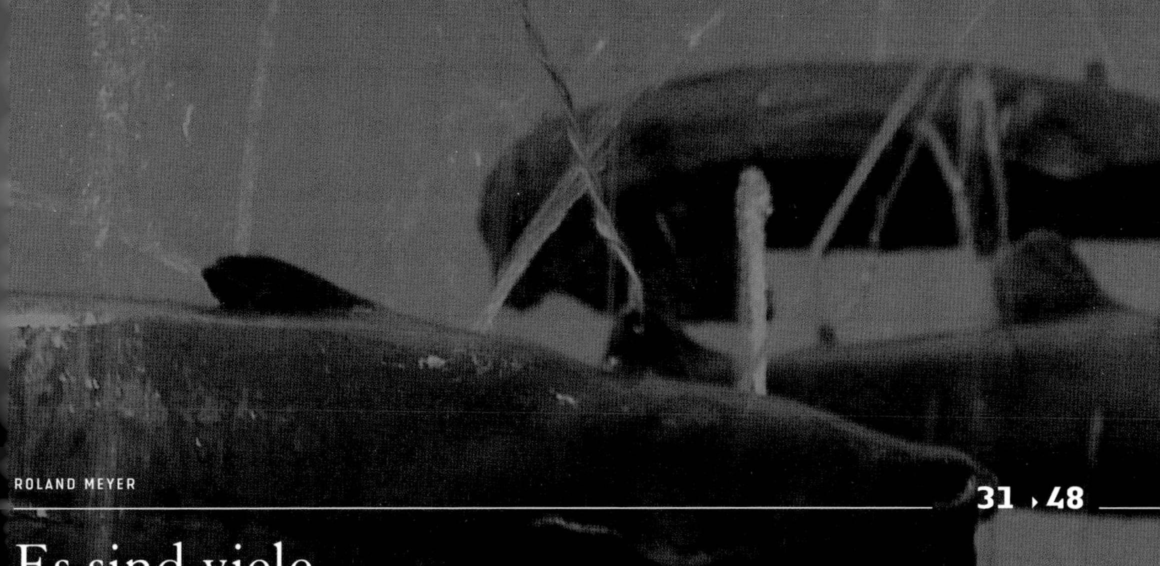

Es sind viele
Anmerkungen zu Bruce Naumans
One Hundred Fish Fountain

ROLAND MEYER

There Are Many of Them
Remarks on Bruce Nauman's
One Hundred Fish Fountain

Es sind viele. Wie viele genau, darüber schwanken die Angaben: Der Titel spricht von einhundert, vermutlich zuverlässigere Quellen wollen bloß 97 gezählt haben. Wie viele also, so könnte man fragen, sind »viele«? Doch zumindest so viele, dass es auf drei mehr oder weniger nicht mehr ankommt. Worauf es vielleicht ankommt: Aus den *Vielen* wird nicht ohne weiteres *Eines,* formt sich keine Gestalt, lässt sich kein Gesamtkörper bilden. Ein Gewimmel, eine unübersichtliche Formation, eine dezentrierte Menge – das führt uns Bruce Nauman in seiner Installation *One Hundred Fish Fountain* vor. Bei den 97 Fischen handelt es sich also nicht um einen Schwarm, sondern um ein offenes Feld, eine ungeordnete Verteilung von Einzelwesen im Raum. Weder gehören sie alle zu derselben Art, noch steuern sie die gleiche Richtung an .... Naumans Kunst hatte bisher zumeist das Individuum im Blick. Der Künstler in der Einsamkeit seines Ateliers, die geschundenen, gefolterten Körper, die Versuchsobjekte behaviouristischer Experimente, die »Betrachter« (die keine ›bloßen‹ Betrachter mehr waren) in den Korridoren der 1970er Jahre – sie alle waren konstitutiv allein, ausgeliefert, isoliert. Und wenn die Figuren in den Videos oder Neonarbeiten einmal zu zweit oder zu mehreren auftraten, dann doch meist in antagonistische Kämpfe verstrickt. *One*

There are many of them. As to exactly how many – well, the opinions vary: The title speaks of one hundred, presumably more reliable sources claim to have counted only ninety-seven. So how many, one could ask, are »many«? In any case so many that three more or less don't matter. What perhaps does matter: Out of the *many* does not automatically arise *one*, no discrete shape becomes apparent, no aggregate body may be formed. A milling mass, a turbulent and confused formation, a multitude brought out of center – this is what Bruce Nauman presents to us in his installation *One Hundred Fish Fountain*. With the ninety-seven fishes it is accordingly a matter, not of a shoal, but of an open field, an unordered distribution of individual beings in space. They neither all belong to one species, nor do all swim in the same direction .... Up to now, Nauman's art has focused mainly on the individual. The artist in the solitude of his studio; the ill-treated, tortured body; the subjects of behavioristic experiments; the »viewers« (who were no longer ›mere‹ viewers) in the corridors of the nineteen-seventies – they were all constitutively alone, exposed, isolated. And when the figures in the videos or neon works at one time or other appeared in groups of two or more, then they were most often involved in antagonistic struggles. *One Hundred Fish Fountain*, however,

Hundred Fish Fountain rückt nun aber eine Art Kollektiv in den Mittelpunkt. Denn die lose im Raum verteilte Menge der in Bronze gegossenen Fischkörper bildet letztlich doch eine Einheit, und zwar nicht durch ihre Form, sondern durch ihre Funktion. Wasser wird in ihr ausgehöhltes Inneres gepumpt, aus jedem der vielfach punktierten Fischleiber spritzen kleine Fontänen zurück ins Bassin. In ihrer Gesamtheit werden sie zu etwas, das der Titel als *Fountain,* als Brunnen oder Fontäne adressiert............................
THE TRUE ARTIST IS AN AMAZING LUMINOUS FOUNTAIN *One Hundred Fish Fountain* verknüpft dabei mehrere Stränge in Naumans Werk. So gehören zum Beispiel die seit den späten 1980er Jahren entstandenen Installationen mit zu Pyramiden aufgetürmten oder an Stahlseilen aufgehängten Tierkörpern in den Einzugsbereich dieser Arbeit. Damals benutzte Nauman taxidermische Rohformen aus Hartplastikschaum, wie sie Tierpräparatoren verwenden: unvollständige, seltsam amorphe, kadaverähnliche Gebilde, die an Hirsche oder Füchse mehr erinnern, als dass sie sie darstellen. Häufig verwendete Nauman nur Teile der Rohformen, setzte sie zu neuen, grotesken Kombinationen zusammen, oder er ließ ihre »Pseudokörper«[01] wie in der Installation *Carousel* (1988) am Boden schleifen, wo ihre mit Graphit bedeckte Oberfläche immer dichter

▸01

now brings to the fore a sort of collective. For the slew of bronze-cast, piscine bodies loosely distributed in space ultimately does constitute a unity, albeit not through their form, but rather through their function. Water is pumped into their hollowed-out interiors and, out of each of the repeatedly punctured piscine bodies, water squirts back into the basin. In their totality, they become something which the title designates as a fountain...
THE TRUE ARTIST IS AN AMAZING LUMINOUS FOUNTAIN *One Hundred Fish Fountain* thereby ties together several strands of Nauman's oeuvre. The installations with animal bodies piled into pyramids or hung from steel cables which have arisen since the late nineteen-eighties, for example, belong to the catchment area of this work. Back then, Nauman employed rough forms out of hard plastic foam such as are used by taxidermists: incomplete, strangely amorphous, cadaverous shapes which offered a vague recollection more than a distinct representation of deer or foxes. Nauman frequently utilized only parts of the rough forms, joined them into new and grotesque combinations, or let their »pseudobodies,«[01] as in the installation *Carousel* (1988), drag along the ground, where their graphite-covered surfaces left behind ever more thick traces. These

werdende Spuren hinterließ. Zweifellos waren diese geschundenen, gequälten Körper auch als Stellvertreter des Menschen zu verstehen, als düstere Exempel für die *conditio humana,* für existenzielle, aber eben auch individuelle Grenzerfahrungen ....
Die bronzenen Fische in der neueren Installation sind dagegen nicht nur vollständig durchgebildet und zoologisch eindeutig identifizierbar, sie wirken trotz ihrer durchlöcherten Körper eher unbeschädigt, ja wie von einer beinahe heiteren Lebendigkeit. Keine düstere Foltermaschine wird hier inszeniert, sondern ein spielerisches Arrangement: ein Wasserspiel, eine vervielfachte Fontäne...
Damit knüpft diese Installation explizit an eine Reihe früherer Arbeiten Naumans an, die den Begriff *Fountain* bereits im Titel tragen. Darunter zwei Fotoarbeiten von 1965 / 66, *Self-Portrait as a Fountain* und *The Artist as a Fountain.* Beide zeigen Nauman, wie er in hohem Bogen Wasser aus dem Mund speit, einmal mit nacktem Oberkörper und erhobenen Händen vor schwarzen Hintergrund posierend, das andere Mal in einem Garten stehend. *The Artist as a Fountain,* das ist das Thema, das Nauman zugleich mit und gegen Marcel Duchamp in mehreren Fotografien und Zeichnungen variiert.[02] *Mit* Duchamp, da er hier offen-

maltreated, tortured bodies were doubtlessly also to be understood as representatives of human beings, as gloomy illustrations of the *conditio humana*, of both existential and individual borderline experiences.......
The bronze fish in the more recent installation, on the other hand, are not only completely shaped and clearly identifiable in zoological terms, but they also convey an undamaged impression in spite of their pierced bodies, exude an almost cheerful vitality. What is staged here is not a mournful torturing device, but instead a playful arrangement: water in zestful motion, a manifold fountain ....
This installation thereby hearkens back to a series of earlier works by Nauman which already include the term »fountain« in their titles. Among these are two photographic works from 1965 / 66, *Self-Portrait as a Fountain* and *The Artist as a Fountain.* Both show Nauman spewing water from his mouth in a high arc, one time posing with naked upper body and raised hands in front of a black background, the other time standing in a garden. *The Artist as a Fountain* – that is the theme which Nauman simultaneously varies, both with and against Marcel Duchamp, in several photographs and drawings.[02] *With* Duchamp, inasmuch as he apparently alludes here to Duchamp's *Fountain*, that iconic ready-made of the inverted urinal which

sichtlich auf Marcel Duchamps *Fountain* anspielt, jenes ikonische Ready-made des umgestülpten Urinals, das Duchamp unter dem Pseudonym R. Mutt einst erfolglos einer Jury zur Ausstellung vorgeschlagen hatte. Und zum Teil auch *gegen* Duchamp, weil Nauman – wenngleich ironisch – als lebende Fontäne gerade jene Künstlerrolle buchstäblich zu verkörpern schien, die schon damals unter Berufung auf eben jene Duchampschen Ready-mades als obsolet verabschiedet worden war: die des Künstlers als Hervorbringer eines originären Werkes, als Schöpfer und Genie...
Vielleicht, so wurde gemutmaßt, zitieren Naumans frühe *Fountains* auch Thomas Carlyles Äußerung über den Dichterfürsten als Helden: »He is a living light-fountain [...] of native original insight, of manhood and heroic nobleness.«[03] Die ikonographische Tradition des Brunnenmotivs kennt aber nicht bloß Künstler-allegorien, sondern in weit umfangreicherer Zahl Szenen der Verkündigung oder auch Darstellungen des Jungbrunnens. Ihnen ist gemein, dass das Wasser des Brunnens Leben spendet. Doch tatsächlich dienen Brunnen neben der überlebenswichtigen Wasserversorgung ebenso als Zierbrunnen, der scheinbar nutz-losen Wasserverschwendung. Im Bild des Brunnens spiegelt sich so auch ein Leben, das über seine eigene

Duchamp, under the pseudonym R. Mutt once unsuccessfully offered to a jury for an exhibition. And to some extent *against* Duchamp, because Nauman – even if ironically – seemed literally to embody as a living fountain precisely that role of the artist which already back then, with reference to precisely those ready-mades of Duchamp, had been declared to be obsolete: namely the celebration of the artist as the producer of an original work, as creator and genius ....
There was speculation as to whether Nauman's early *Fountains* also referred to Thomas Carlyle's description of the prince among poets as a hero: »He is a living light-fountain [...] of native original insight, of man-hood and heroic nobleness.«[03] The iconographic tradition of the fountain motif involves not only allegories of artists but, in far greater number, scenes of the annunciation or also representations of the Fountain of Youth. Common to them all is the belief that the water of the fountain is life-giving. But in fact fountains, in addition to the provision of water that is so important for survival, also serve as decorative devices in a seemingly useless waste of water. Hence mirrored in the image of the fountain is also a life which points past its own limitations, beyond that which is merely necessary to preserve life. »The cistern contains: the

Begrenztheit, über das bloß Lebensnotwendige hinausweist. »The cistern contains, the fountain overflows«, so lautet eines von William Blakes »Proverbs of Hell«.[04] Ebenso wie das noch berühmtere »Exuberance is Beauty« feiert es den Überfluss und wendet sich gegen das Ideal der Mäßigung, wie es die traditionelle Lebenskunst seit der Antike bestimmt hatte. Vermutlich ist auch hier vor allem das Künstlerindividuum als exzessiver *Fountain* gemeint. Der romantische Typus des *poète maudit* zumindest, der sich selbst, sein Leben und sein Talent in einem Akt heldenhafter Verausgabung verschwendet, findet sich in Blakes Sentenz vorgeprägt. War für Blake und vor allem für seine Nachfolger jedoch die Idee der Verausgabung deshalb so attraktiv, weil sie das irrationale Gegenstück zur Rationalität des bürgerlichen *homo oeconomicus* darstellte, der mit seinen Ressourcen und Fähigkeiten haushält und stets auf die Maximierung des eigenen Nutzens spekulierte, so sollte im 20. Jahrhundert Georges Bataille in *La parte maudite*[05] die geheime Ratio der Verausgabung offenbaren. Denn jedes System, sei es biologisch oder sozial, so lautete Batailles Intuition, ist stets von einem konstitutiven Überschuss an Energie geprägt – und so sind scheinbar irrationale Akte der Verschwendung tatsächlich unabdingbar, denn sie dienen in Wahrheit der Stabilität des Systems.

fountain overflows« is one of William Blake's »Proverbs of Hell« from *The Marriage of Heaven and Hell*.[04] Just like the even more famous proverb »Exuberance is Beauty,« it celebrates excess and opposes the ideal of moderation such as had been propagated as an ideal since Antiquity in the traditional art of living. Presumably the reference here is also to the artistic individual as an excessively flowing fountain. Blake's maxim anticipates the Romantic topos of the *poète maudit* who, in an act of heroic self-expenditure, burns out himself, his life and his talent. Blake and especially his successors, however, found the idea of self-dissipation so appealing because it represented the irrational opposite to the plodding reasonableness of the bourgeois *homo oeconomicus*, who used his resources and capabilities frugally and constantly speculated so as to derive the maximum benefit for himself, in the twentieth century Georges Bataille would reveal the secret ratio of self-expenditure in *La parte maudite*.[05] For according to Bataille's intuition, every system, be it biological or social, is always marked by a constitutive excess of energy – and thus seemingly irrational acts of wastefulness are actually essential, for in fact they serve the stability of the system. Magnificent celebrations, profligate luxury, just as religion and art and also wars, are from Bataille's point of view nothing

Rauschende Feste, verschwenderischer Luxus, ebenso Religion und Kunst, aber auch Kriege sind aus Sicht Batailles daher nichts anderes als produktive oder destruktive Formen der Verausgabung überschüssiger Energie. Wahrhaft irrational, weil in letzter Konsequenz verheerende Folgen zeitigend, ist also bloß die individuelle Kosten-Nutzen-Maximierung der beschränkten – im Gegensatz zu Batailles »allgemeiner« – Ökonomie. Kunst als Akt der Verschwendung von Energie und Ressourcen wird jedoch selten so anschaulich wie im nutzlosen Wasserspiel. Nicht von ungefähr diente es seit dem Manierismus in den Gärten des Adels der Zurschaustellung von Reichtum und Pracht, als Form ostentativen Konsums ....

ZIRKULATION ALS INSTALLATION Nach Duchamps *Fountain* müssen wir, so lautet ein verbreitetes Argument, die Rolle des Künstlers nicht mehr als die eines Produzenten, sondern nur mehr als die eines privilegierten Konsumenten begreifen. Mit dem Ready-made wird Kunst zur Praxis der Selektion, oder, wie es Beat Wyss jüngst systemtheoretisch reformuliert hat, zur »zweiten Beobachtung«. Künstlerinnen und Künstler bilden nicht mehr die Welt ab – sie wählen vielmehr aus der Welt aus, was sie dem Publikum zur ästhetischen Betrachtung anbieten. Sie stellen mithin ihre eigenen Auswahlkriterien im Kunstraum zur Diskussion.

other than productive or destructive forms of the expenditure of excess energy. What is truly irrational, because ultimately leading to disastrous consequences, is in fact the individual cost-benefit maximization of the limited – in contrast to Bataille's »general« – economy. Art as an act of wasting energy and resources, however, is seldom so evident as in a useless fountain. Not by chance has it served in the gardens of the aristocracy ever since Mannerism for the display of wealth and magnificence, as a form of ostentatious consumption ....

CIRCULATION AS INSTALLATION According to a widespread argument, after Duchamp's *Fountain* we are compelled to understand the role of the artist, not any longer as that of a producer, but only as that of a privileged consumer. With the ready-made, art becomes a practice of selection or, as Beat Wyss recently called it in a systems-theoretical reformulation, a »second observation.« Artists no longer depict the world – instead they select from the world that which they then offer to the public for aesthetic contemplation. They consequently open for discussion their own criteria of selection in the artistic space. They make it possible for us to learn to see in a new manner, from the perspective of art, the things of this

Sie erlauben es, die Dinge der Welt, die Welt der Waren ebenso wie die Bildwelten aus Wissenschaft und Alltagskultur unter der Perspektive der Kunst neu sehen zu lernen.[06].. Kunst als zweite Beobachtung ist daher nur möglich vor dem Hintergrund eines ausdifferenzierten Kunstsystems, auf der Basis auch territorial differenzierter Orte der Kunst: Museen, Kunstvereine, Galerien. Kunstwerke zeigen sich dabei an diesen Orten, das hat Boris Groys in seiner *Topologie der Kunst* beschrieben, immer bereits als Installationen, auch wo es sich dem Anschein nach noch um klassische Gattungen wie Malerei handelt. Denn wenn jedes Kunstwerk auch Ware ist, aber keinesfalls jede Ware auch ein Kunstwerk, dann ist es erst die dauerhafte Installation, die die Ware zum Werk macht.[07] Ästhetische Erfahrung wird möglich, wo die Zirkulation stillgelegt wird, die Dinge dem ökonomischen Kreislauf entzogen werden. So allgemein solche Überlegungen scheinen, so konkret ist ihr Bezug zu jenem Werk, um das es hier gehen soll. Denn *One Hundred Fish Fountain* ist, wie letztlich jeder (Zier-)Brunnen, die Inszenierung der Zirkulation als Installation, als technisch erzeugter und betriebener Wasserkreislauf. Es ist also gleichsam ein Modell der Zirkulation, ein in sich geschlossenes symbolisches System im Innern des sozialen Systems Kunst.

world – the world of commodities as well as the pictorial worlds from science and everyday culture.[06] Art as a second observation is hence only possible against the background of a finely differentiated art system, on the basis also of territorially differentiated sites of art: museums, galleries, art associations. Thus works of art always already present themselves at these sites – this has been described by Boris Groys in his *Topologie der Kunst* – as installations, even when it is apparently still a matter of classical genres such as painting. For if every work of art is also a commodity, but every commodity is in no way also a work of art, then it is first the enduring installation which transforms the commodity into a work of art.[07] Aesthetic experience becomes possible there where circulation is brought to a standstill, where objects are removed from economic flow. As general as such considerations seem, so concrete is their relationship to that work which is the focus of attention here. For *One Hundred Fish Fountain* is, just as is ultimately the case with every (decorative) fountain, the staging of circulation as installation, as a technically produced and operated circular flow of water. It is thus, as it were, a model of circulation, a closed symbolic system within the social system of art..

Dass sie auf Zirkulation basieren, das verbindet etwa das ökonomische System mit biologischen und ökologischen Systemen. Genauer: Der Begriff der Zirkulation beschrieb das System der Verteilung von Flüssigkeiten in Kreisläufen, lange bevor er auf die Formen des Verkehrs von Menschen, Geld, Waren und Ideen übertragen wurde. Der Kunstkritiker Jörg Heiser hat jüngst darauf hingewiesen, dass sich dieser Wandel der Zirkulation »vom physischen Phänomen zur ökonomischen Metapher«[08] beispielhaft im Werk Hans Haackes aus den 1960er und 1970er Jahren spiegelt: Haackes Weg führte ihn von Arbeiten wie dem *Condensation Cube* (1963–1965), in dem Wasser flüssig und als Wasserdampf in einem minimalistischen Glaskubus zirkulierte, zum *Manet-Projekt '74,* das die Geschichte einer ganz speziellen Zirkulation auf dem Kunstmarkt nachzeichnete, nämlich die Provenienz von Edouard Manets *Spargel-Stillleben* (1880). Für die Zirkulationsprozesse, nicht nur von Kunst und Kapital (die er bekanntlich in einer berühmt gewordenen Gleichung als Äquivalente postuliert hatte), interessierte sich in den 1970er Jahren auch Joseph Beuys. Seine *Honigpumpe am Arbeitsplatz,* 1977 auf der *documenta 6* installiert, war dabei explizit als organisches Gesellschaftsmodell gedacht. Als anthropomorphes System der Zirkulation von Energie sollte sie, begleitet von

The fact that they are all based upon circulation connects the economic system, for instance, with biological and ecological systems. More precisely – the notion of circulation described the pattern of the distribution of liquids in closed systems long before it was applied to the forms of transportation for people, money, commodities and ideas. The art critic Jörg Heiser has recently pointed out that this shift of circulation »from a physical phenomenon to an economic metaphor«[08] is mirrored in an exemplary manner in the works of Hans Haacke from the nineteen-sixties and -seventies: Haacke's developmental path led him from works such as the *Condensation Cube* (1963–65), in which water circulated in both liquid and gaseous form in a minimalist glass cube, to *Manet-Projekt '74,* which traced the history of a quite special circulation in the art market, namely the provenance of Edouard Manet's *A Bunch of Asparagus* (1880). In the nineteen-seventies, Joseph Beuys also showed an interest in the circulation processes of not only art and capital (which he postulated as equivalent in a famous equation). His *Honigpumpe am Arbeitsplatz* (Honey Pump at the Workplace, 1977), installed at the *documenta 6,* was explicitly conceived as an organic model of society. As an anthropomorphic system of the circulation of energy, it was intended,

40

den Aktivitäten der »Freien Internationalen Universität«, Beuys' Konzept der »sozialen Plastik« veranschaulichen ....

Systeme konstituieren sich durch operationale Schließung. *One Hundred Fish Fountain* als System zu betrachten, heißt daher zunächst, es von seiner Umwelt zu unterscheiden. Die Umwelt, das wäre das Museum oder die Galerie, die hier, wie in diesem Fall die kestnergesellschaft, in einem sehr handfesten Sinne als Support-System dient. Zum Erhalt der Zirkulation werden aus dieser Umwelt beständig Energie und Ressourcen in das System eingespeist (ein Zusammenhang, den die Systemtheorie die »strukturelle Kopplung« von System und Umwelt nennt).[09] Der Großteil des Wassers wird dabei mittels Umwälzpumpen in Zirkulation gehalten – verschwendet wird neben der Energie, die für den Betrieb nötig ist, auch das Wasser, das durch Verdunstung entweicht. Denn anders als bei Haackes *Condensation Cube* zirkuliert das Wasser in *One Hundred Fish Fountain* nicht im hermetischen Kubus, sondern gleichsam im Offenen.[10] ....

Vor allem aber handelt es sich um einen Kreislauf mit verteilten Akteuren – jeder der beinahe hundert

along with the activities of the »Freie Internationale Universität,« to demonstrate Beuys' concept of the »social plastic« ....

Systems constitute themselves through operational closure. Observing *One Hundred Fish Fountain* as a system accordingly means first of all differentiating it from its surroundings. The environment would be the museum or gallery, in this case the kestnergesellschaft, which serves in a quite concrete sense as a support system. In order to maintain circulation, energies and resources are constantly injected into the system (a connection which systems theory calls the »structural coupling« of system and environment).[09] A good portion of the water is thereby maintained in circulation by means of pumps – wasted along with the energy necessary for their operation is also the water which escapes through evaporation. For in contrast to Haacke's *Condensation Cube*, the water in *One Hundred Fish Fountain* does not flow through a hermetic cube, but out in the open, as it were.[10] ....

Above all, however, it is a matter of circulation with distributed protagonists – each of the almost hundred fish participates in the even distribution of liquid in the overall system. So the circulation of water in

Fische partizipiert an der gleichmäßigen Verteilung der Flüssigkeit im Gesamtsystem. Die Zirkulation des Wassers in Naumans *One Hundred Fish Fountain* führt also auf eine sehr buchstäbliche Weise die Aktivität einer Vielheit von Elementen zurück auf das eine, ihnen gemeinsame Medium ....

ZERFALL UND NEUBEGINN Vor dem Hintergrund der früheren Arbeiten zum *Fountain*-Komplex betrachtet, wird nun deutlich, was vielleicht die entscheidende Setzung Naumans in dieser neuen Installation ausmacht: die Ersetzung des Künstler-Ichs durch eine Tier-Vielheit. An die Stelle der ironischen Buchstäblichkeit, mit der der junge Nauman das Künstlerindividuum als Quelle des Sinns verkörperte, tritt ein System, in dem zunächst keine einzige Quelle mehr auszumachen ist. Jeder einzelne Fisch ist ein Multiplikator, eine Art Verteilerknoten in einem Netzwerk ....

Das Ergebnis ist ein fortlaufender Prozess der Aufteilung und erneuten Sammlung, der Differenzierung und Vermischung – die immer annährend gleich bleibende Menge Wasser wird aus einem Bassin in beinahe hundert Fische gepumpt, durch an die tausend Öffnungen hinausgeschossen, um anschließend wieder aufgefangen und vereint zu werden. Es entsteht ein Schauspiel scheinbar unaufhörlicher Bewegung, die

▶09 ▶10

Nauman's *One Hundred Fish Fountain* thus refers in a quite literal manner the activity of a multiplicity of elements back to the one medium common to them all...

DECAY AND RENEWAL Viewed against the background of the early works on the *Fountain* complex, it now becomes clear what perhaps constitutes Nauman's decisive act in this new installation, namely the replacement of the artist's self with a multitude of animals. In place of the ironical literalness with which the young Nauman embodied the artistic individual as the source of meaning, there emerges a system in which at first no single source may any longer be identified. Each separate fish is a multiplier, a sort of distribution node in a network ....

The result is an ongoing process of distribution and renewed collection, of differentiation and amalgamation – the almost constant amount of water is pumped out of a basin into close to a hundred fish, spewed out of nearly a thousand openings, then captured and commingled once again. There arises the spectacle of a seemingly incessant movement which, however, always circles around itself, doesn't get anywhere, but only repeats the same thing: a loop on an elementary level, so to say...

jedoch immer nur um sich selber kreist, nicht vom Fleck kommt, die Wiederholung des Immergleichen: ein *loop* auf gleichsam elementarer Ebene..
Doch bricht der Strom immer wieder ab, die Quelle versiegt, nur noch Tropfen rinnen aus den hohlen, perforierten Fischleibern. Fast scheint es, als hätte das Support-System versagt, als sei die Energiezufuhr unterbrochen. In den alternierenden Perioden, in denen die Pumpen das Wasserspiel in Betrieb setzen und es anschließend erneut aussetzen, kommt es immer wieder zu Momenten, in denen fast die gesamte Wassermenge der Zirkulation entzogen wird, nur noch einzelne Tropfen an den Fischen hängen, während sich die überwiegende Menge im Bassin sammelt. Im Wechsel von *On* und *Off* zeigen sich die einzelnen Fische mal als Teil eines funktionierenden Systems, mal als isolierte, relativ unverbundene Elemente in einer losen Anordnung. Und wie immer, wenn es nicht weitergeht, wird gerade im Moment des Zusammenbruchs des Systems offensichtlich, wie sehr sein Funktionieren auf die Unterstützung von Außen angewiesen war. In *Masse und Macht* hat Elias Cannetti den Streik als den Moment charakterisiert, in dem die bloß fiktive, durch die faktische Arbeitsteilung konterkarierte Gleichheit der Arbeiter zu einer Wirklichen wird:

Yet the flow is disrupted again and again; the source dries up, and only drops descend from the empty, perforated piscine bodies. It almost seems as if the support system had failed, as if the injection of energy had been interrupted. During the alternating periods in which the pumps set in motion the play of water and subsequently cancel it once again, there are repeated moments in which almost the entire amount of circulating water has been removed and only individual drops hang from the fishes, while the preponderant part is collected in the basin. In this alternation of »on« and »off,« the individual fishes are sometimes parts of a functioning system, sometimes isolated, relatively unconnected elements in a loose arrangement. And just as always, when things don't go any further, it becomes clear in the very moment of the system's breakdown to how great an extent its functioning was dependent on support from outside.........................
In *Masse und Macht*, Elias Canetti characterized the strike as the moment when the merely fictional equality of the workers, thwarted by the actual distribution of labor, becomes a real equality: »When they stop working, they all do the same thing.«[11] Things are reversed here – as soon as the fishes stop spewing, the differences become apparent, the system collapses into its individual components. In contrast to Beuys'

»Wenn sie die Arbeit niederlegen, tun alle dasselbe.«[11] Hier ist es umgekehrt – sobald die Fische aufhören zu sprudeln, fallen die Unterschiede ins Auge, zerfällt das System in seine individuellen Bestandteile. Anders als in Beuys' kontinuierlich arbeitender *Honigpumpe* entsteht also keine dauerhafte organische Einheit, vielmehr kippt der Versuchsaufbau beständig zwischen Vereinzelung und Systembildung, baut sich ein Zusammenhang auf, der sich stets aufs Neue als gefährdet erweist. Der Zirkulation, das zeigt sich gerade da, wo sie aussetzt, kann stets die Grundlage entzogen werden, gibt es doch *einen* Motor, der alles vorantreibt und an dem alles hängt. Mit Gilles Deleuze und Felix Guattari ließe sich hier von Prozessen der *Deterritorialisierung* und *Reterritorialisierung* sprechen, von einer Fluchtlinie in die unbestimmte Vielheit, die immer wieder auf eine identische Einheit zurückgebogen wird. Nur muss offen bleiben, inwiefern diese Einheit überhaupt identisch bleibt. Es ist dies eine der ältesten Frage der Philosophie. Gibt es Stabilität im Werden? Ist also letztlich die Einheit der sichtbaren Vielheit vorgängig? Auf solche ontologischen Fragen gibt Naumans Arbeit keineswegs eine eindeutige Antwort. Vielmehr stehen sich in *One Hundred Fish Fountain* zwei mögliche Weltmodelle gegenüber – nicht versöhnt, sondern im schärfsten Kontrast. So wird

continuously working *Honigpumpe*, there arises no enduring, organic unity, but instead the experimental structure switches continuously between separation and system building; an interconnection establishes itself, only to become endangered anew. The circulation – this becomes clear precisely at the point when it ceases – can have its basis removed, inasmuch as there is *one* motor which drives everything onward and upon which everything depends. With Gilles Deleuze and Felix Guattari it would be possible to speak here about processes of *deterritorialization* and *reterritorialization*, about a vanishing-line into an indefinite multiplicity which is repeatedly bent back round to an identical unity. But the question must remain open as to the degree to which this unity actually remains identical. This is one of the oldest questions in philosophy. Is there a stability in becoming? Is unity ultimately antecedent to visible multiplicity? Nauman's work provides no unambiguous answer to this sort of ontological question. Instead two possible world models stand opposite one another in *One Hundred Fish Fountain* – not reconciled, but existing in the sharpest contrast. Thus no final state is attained in eternal repetition; each decision is postponed indefinitely. Consequently, a specific suspense proves to be a structural characteristic of this work. For suspense is the

_44_

in der ewigen Wiederholung kein endgültiger Zustand erreicht, jegliche Entscheidung auf unbestimmte Zeit aufgeschoben. Ein spezifischer *Suspense* erweist sich mithin als Strukturmerkmal dieser Arbeit. Denn *Suspense,* das ist eben jene Spannung, die sich einstellt, wo die Dinge in der Schwebe gehalten, mithin suspendiert werden – aufgeschoben meint hier letztlich auch aufgehoben. Nicht nur die Fische hängen also, an Drähten befestigt, buchstäblich in der Luft. Auch das Verhältnis von Einzelnem und Menge, von isolierten Elementen und Systemzusammenhang verbleibt in einer Balance, die prekär erscheint, weil sie ständig kippt und sich zugleich gerade in der endlosen Wiederholung dieses Kippmoments als stabil erweist...

Naumans *One Hundred Fish Fountain,* so die Lesart, die hier vorgeschlagen werden soll, ist ein bewusst mehrdeutiges Modell von sozialen wie ästhetischen, ja vielleicht sogar universalen Prozessen der Vervielfachung und Vereinzelung, der Strukturbildung und Auflösung, der Zirkulation und Unterbrechung. Doch anders als etwa die Modellbildungen der Wissenschaft erschöpft sich Naumans Arbeit nicht in der

tension which arises when things are held in abeyance, in suspension – here to be postponed ultimately also means to be raised and overridden. Not only the fishes, attached to wires, literally hang in mid-air. Also the relationship between individual and multitude, between isolated elements and systemic interconnection, remains in an equilibrium which seems precarious because it constantly oscillates and simultaneously proves to be stable, precisely in the endless repetition of this aspect of alternation ....

In the reading suggested here, Nauman's *One Hundred Fish Fountain* is a deliberately ambiguous model of both social and aesthetic, perhaps even universal processes of increase and isolation, of structural formation and dissolution, of circulation and interruption. But in contrast, for example, to the models set up by the sciences, Nauman's work does not exhaust itself in the depiction of processes about which one assumes that they remain extrinsic to the specific materiality of the model and hence could be likewise represented in

Veranschaulichung von Abläufen, von denen man annimmt, sie blieben der spezifischen Materialität des Modells äußerlich und ließen sich daher auch ebenso in anderer Weise darstellen. Vielmehr macht Nauman das Modell selbst zum Gegenstand ästhetischer Erfahrung. Dies ist den Strategien weit jüngerer Künstler nicht unähnlich, die zum Beispiel Modelle aus den Naturwissenschaften in raumgreifende Installationen übersetzen oder den Ausstellungsraum zum Schauplatz ebenso ausgetüftelter wie letztlich absurder Produktionsprozesse machen. Bräuchte es noch eine Begründung für Naumans über Jahrzehnte hinweg unangefochtene Position in der Gegenwartskunst, dann fände sie sich in der fast spielerischen Leichtigkeit, mit der er solche Zeitgenossenschaft in der Neuinterpretation bereits etablierter Parameter seines Werkes herzustellen vermag: In einem Prozess steter Differenzierung, der aus einem ebenso unerschöpflich scheinenden wie doch stets wieder erkennbaren Vorrat an Formen und Themen gespeist wird. Damit wird *One Hundred Fish Fountain* mit seiner prekären Balance zwischen Wiederholung und stetem Neuanfang auch zu einem Modell künstlerischer Praxis, ja vielleicht sogar zu einem versteckten Selbstporträt....................

another manner. Instead Nauman makes the model itself the object of aesthetic experience. This is not dissimilar to the strategies of much younger artists who, for example, transfer models from the natural sciences into space-encompassing installations or turn the exhibition space into the scene of elaborately worked-out and ultimately absurd production processes. If justification were required for Nauman's prominent position in contemporary art, uncontested for decades by now, then it could be found in the almost playful lightness with which he is capable of creating such contemporaneity in the reinterpretation of the already established parameters of his work: in a process of constant differentiation that is nourished by a supply of forms and themes which both seems to be inexhaustible yet remains constantly recognizable. In this way *One Hundred Fish Fountain*, with its precarious balance between repetition and constant renewal, also becomes a model of artistic practice, perhaps even a concealed self-portrait...

▶ 01 Robert Hughes: *Bilder von Amerika. Die amerikanische Kunst von den Anfängen bis zur Gegenwart.* München 1997, S. 577 ▶ 02 Zu nennen wären hier noch die Skizze *Myself As a Marble Fountain* (1967) und der Entwurf für einen Fensterrahmen mit der Inschrift *The True Artist is an Amazing Luminous Fountain* (1966). Vgl. Coosje van Bruggen: *Bruce Nauman.* Basel 1988, S. 15 sowie Abb. S. 48, 49 und 121 ▶ 03 Zit. nach Eckhard Neuman: *Künstlermythen. Eine psycho-historische Studie über Kreativität.* Frankfurt/New York 1986, S. 85. Noch ein weiteres Vorbild liesse sich finden, wird Nauman doch hier buchstäblich selbst zum *Fountainhead* – so lautet nämlich der Titel eines Romans der konservativen, russisch-amerikanischen Radikalkapitalistin Ayn Rand, der vom ungebrochenen Willen eines modernistischen Hochhausarchitekten handelt und als einer der weltweit erfolgreichsten Künstlerromane überhaupt gilt. 1949 wurde er unter der Regie von King Vidor verfilmt, mit Gary Cooper in der Hauptrolle. Vgl. Ayn Rand. *The Fountainhead.* New York 1996 (erstmals 1946) ▶ 04 Zit. nach Ernst Bloch: *Philosophische Ansicht des Künstlerromans.* In ders.: *Literarische Aufsätze. Werkausgabe Band 9,* Frankfurt am Main 1985, S. 263–276. Hier: S. 273. Vgl. zu den *Proverbs of Hell.* Auch: Michael Davis: *William Blake. A New Kind of Man.* Berkeley/Los Angeles 1977, S. 58 ff ▶ 05 Erstveröffentlichung 1949; dt. als: Georges Bataille: *Der verfemte*

▶ 01 Robert Hughes: *Bilder von Amerika. Die amerikanische Kunst von den Anfängen bis zur Gegenwart* (American Visions: The Epic History of Art in America). Munich 1997, p. 577 ▶ 02 Worthy of mention here are the sketch *Myself as a Marble Fountain* (1967) and the design for a windowframe with the inscription *The True Artist is an Amazing Luminous Fountain* (1966). Cf. Coosje van Bruggen: *Bruce Nauman.* Basel 1988, p. 15 as well as illus. pp. 48, 49 and 121 ▶ 03 Quoted from Eckhard Neuman: *Künstlermythen. Eine psycho-historische Studie über Kreativität* (Myths of Artists. A Psycho-Historical Study of Creativity). Frankfurt am Main/New York 1986, p. 85. A further model may be found, inasmuch as Nauman himself literally becomes a *Fountainhead* – this is the title of a novel by the conservative Russian-American, radical capitalist Ayn Rand, a work which celebrates the unbroken will of an architect of Modernist skyscrapers and is regarded as one of the most successful novels about artists in the world. It was filmed in 1949, directed by King Vidor with Gary Cooper in the leading role. Cf. Ayn Rand: *The Fountainhead.* New York 1996 (first published in 1946) ▶ 04 Quoted from Ernst Bloch: *Philosophische Ansicht des Künstlerromans* (Philosophical View of the Artist-Novel), in ibid.: *Literarische Aufsätze. Werkausgabe Band 9* (Literary Essays, Complete Works Vol. 9). Frankfurt am Main 1985, pp. 263–276. Here p. 273. Cf. with regard to the *Proverbs of Hell* also Michael Davis: *William Blake. A New Kind of Man.* Berkeley/Los Angeles 1977, p. 58 ff ▶ 05 First published in French in 1949; in German as: Georges Bataille: *Der verfemte Teil. Versuch einer allgemeinen Ökomomie* (Georges

Teil. Versuch einer allgemeinen Ökonomie. In Ders.: *Die Aufhebung der Ökonomie*. München 2001 ▶ **06** Vgl. Beat Wyss: *Vom Bild zum Kunstsystem*. 2 Bde., Köln 2005 ▶ **07** Vgl. Boris Groys: *Topologie der Kunst*. München/Wien 2003 ▶ **08** Jörg Heiser: *Plötzlich diese Übersicht. Was gute zeitgenössische Kunst ausmacht*. Berlin 2007, S. 311 ▶ **09** Für eine ausführliche, systemtheoretische Deutung der Rauminstallationen Naumans vgl. auch Hans Dieter Huber: *Erlernte Hilflosigkeit. Rauminstallationen von Bruce Nauman*. In: Holger Birkholz u.a. (Hrsg.): *Zeitgenössische Kunst und Kunstwissenschaft. Zur Aktualisierung ihres Verhältnisses*. Weimar 1995, S. 104–125 ▶ **10** Während also bei Haackes *Condensation Cube* die Verdunstung die *physischen* Bedingungen des Galerieraums (nämlich die in ihm herrschende Temperatur) sichtbar macht, lässt sich das Wechselspiel von Verdunstung und Wiederauffüllung in Naumans Arbeit als subtiler Kommentar zu den *institutionellen* Bedingungen des Kunstraums lesen. Zu den damit verbundenen unterschiedlichen Formen von *site-specificity* vgl. Miwon Kwon: *One Place After Another. Site-Specific Art and Local Identity*. Cambridge (MA)/London 2004, v.a. S. 11–31 ▶ **11** Elias Canetti: *Masse und Macht*. Frankfurt am Main 1992 (Sonderausgabe, erstmals: Hildesheim 1960), S. 58 ....

Bataille, The Accursed Share: An Essay on General Economy). In ibid.: *Die Aufhebung der Ökonomie* (The Sublation of Economy). Munich 2001 ▶ **06** Cf. Beat Wyss: *Vom Bild zum Kunstsystem* (From Image to Art System). 2 vols., Cologne 2005 ▶ **07** Cf. Boris Groys: *Topologie der Kunst* (Topology of Art). Munich/Vienna 2003 ▶ **08** Jörg Heiser: *Plötzlich diese Übersicht. Was gute zeitgenössische Kunst ausmacht* (Suddenly this overview. What constitutes good contemporary art). Berlin 2007, p. 311 ▶ **09** For a detailed, systems-theoretical interpretation of Nauman's spatial installations, cf. also Hans Dieter Huber: *Erlernte Hilflosigkeit. Rauminstallationen von Bruce Nauman* (Learned Helplessness. Spatial Installations by Bruce Nauman). in: Holger Birkholz et al. (editors). *Zeitgenössische Kunst und Kunstwissenschaft. Zur Aktualisierung ihres Verhältnisses* (Contemporary Art and Art Scholarship. On Bringing Their Relation Up-To-Date). Weimar 1995, pp. 104–125 ▶ **10** Thus while in Haacke's *Condensation Cube* the evaporation brings to light the *physical* conditions of the gallery space (namely its temperature), in Nauman's work the interplay between evaporation and replenishment may be read as a subtle commentary on the *institutional* conditions of the art space. Concerning the concomitant, diverse forms of *site specificity,* cf. Miwon Kwon: *One Place After Another. Site-Specific Art and Local Identity*. Cambridge (MA)/London 2004, pp. 11–31 ▶ **11** Elias Canetti: *Masse und Macht* (Crowds and Power). Frankfurt am Main 1992 (special edition: first published Hildesheim 1960), p. 58 ....

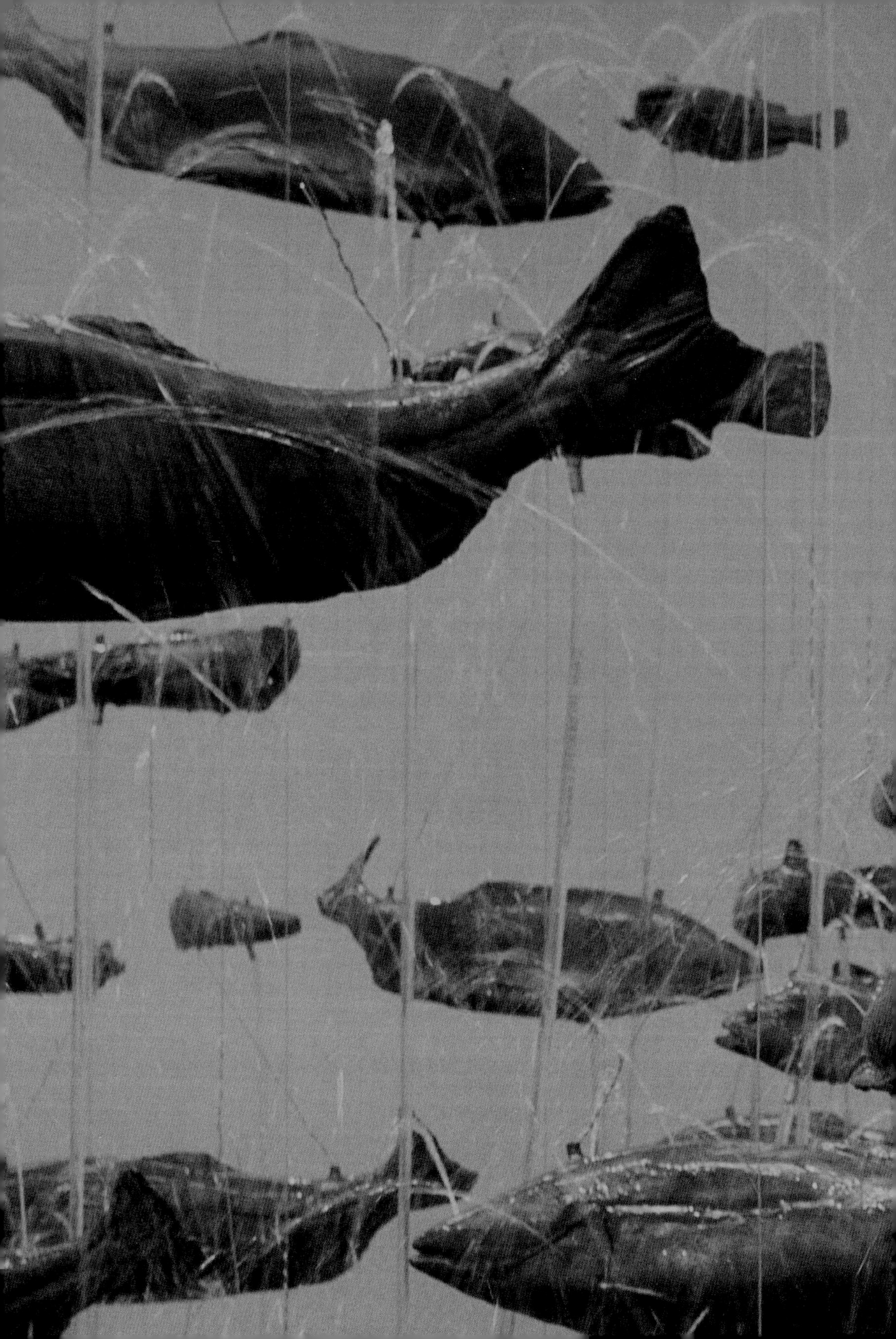

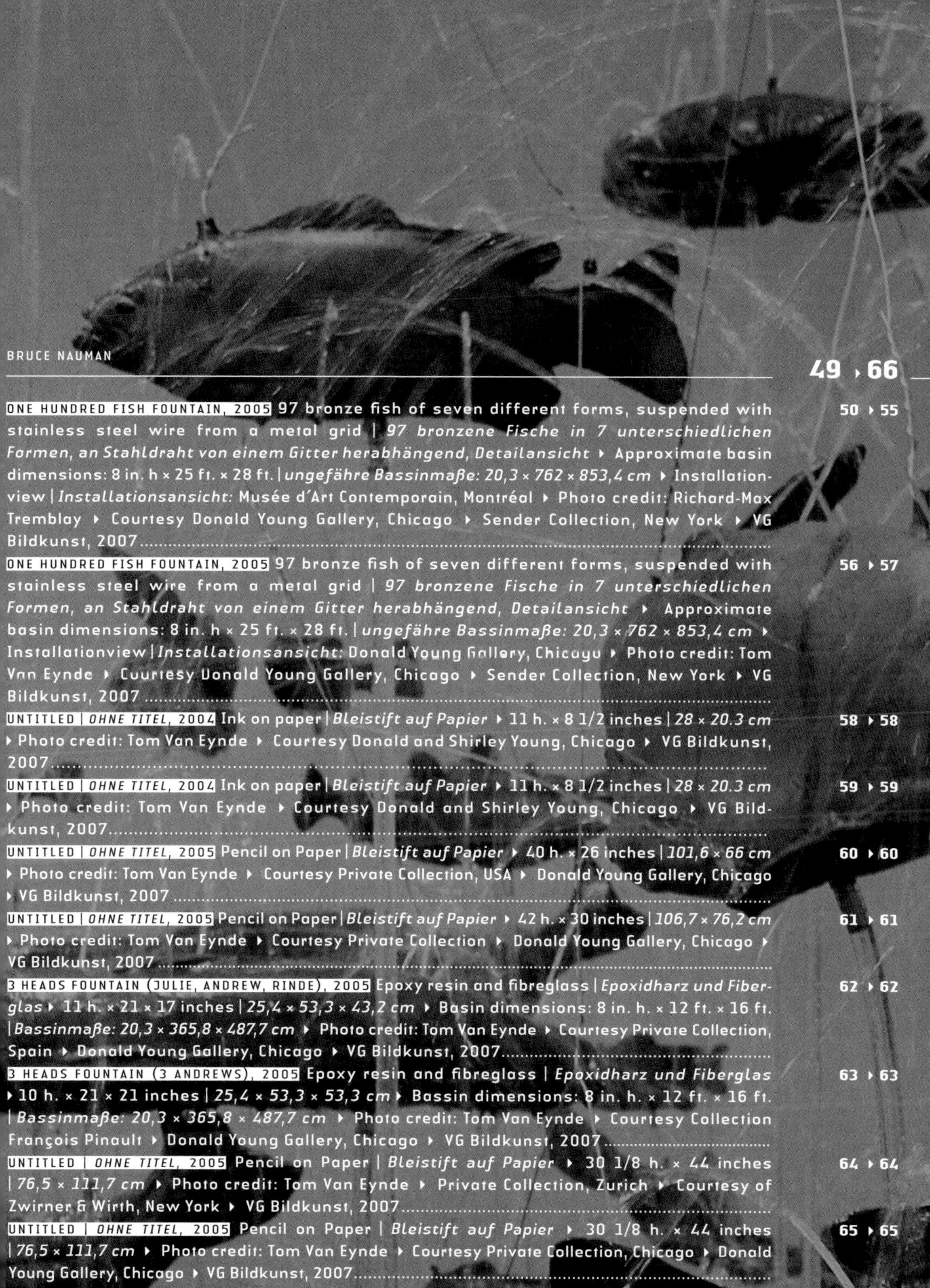

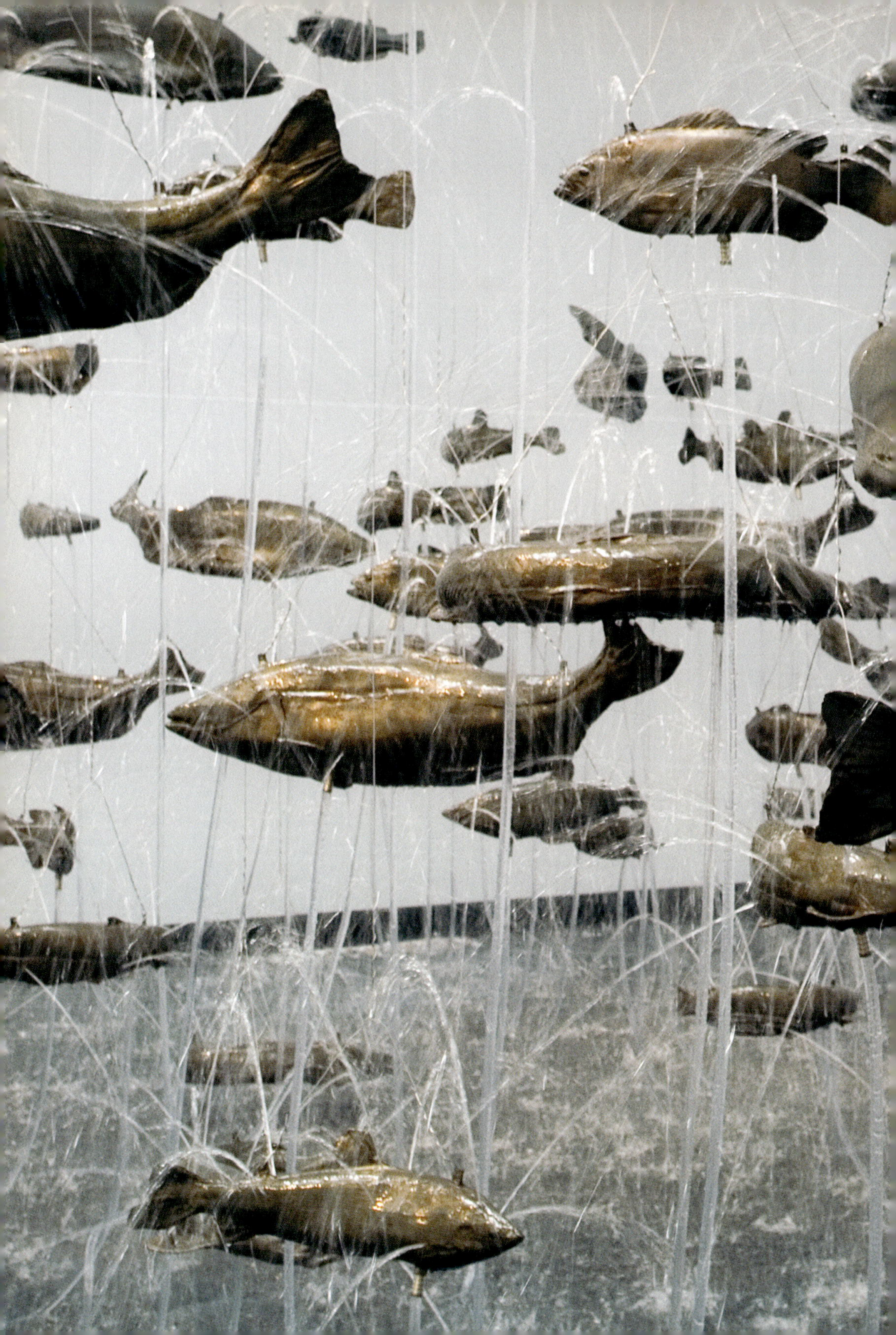

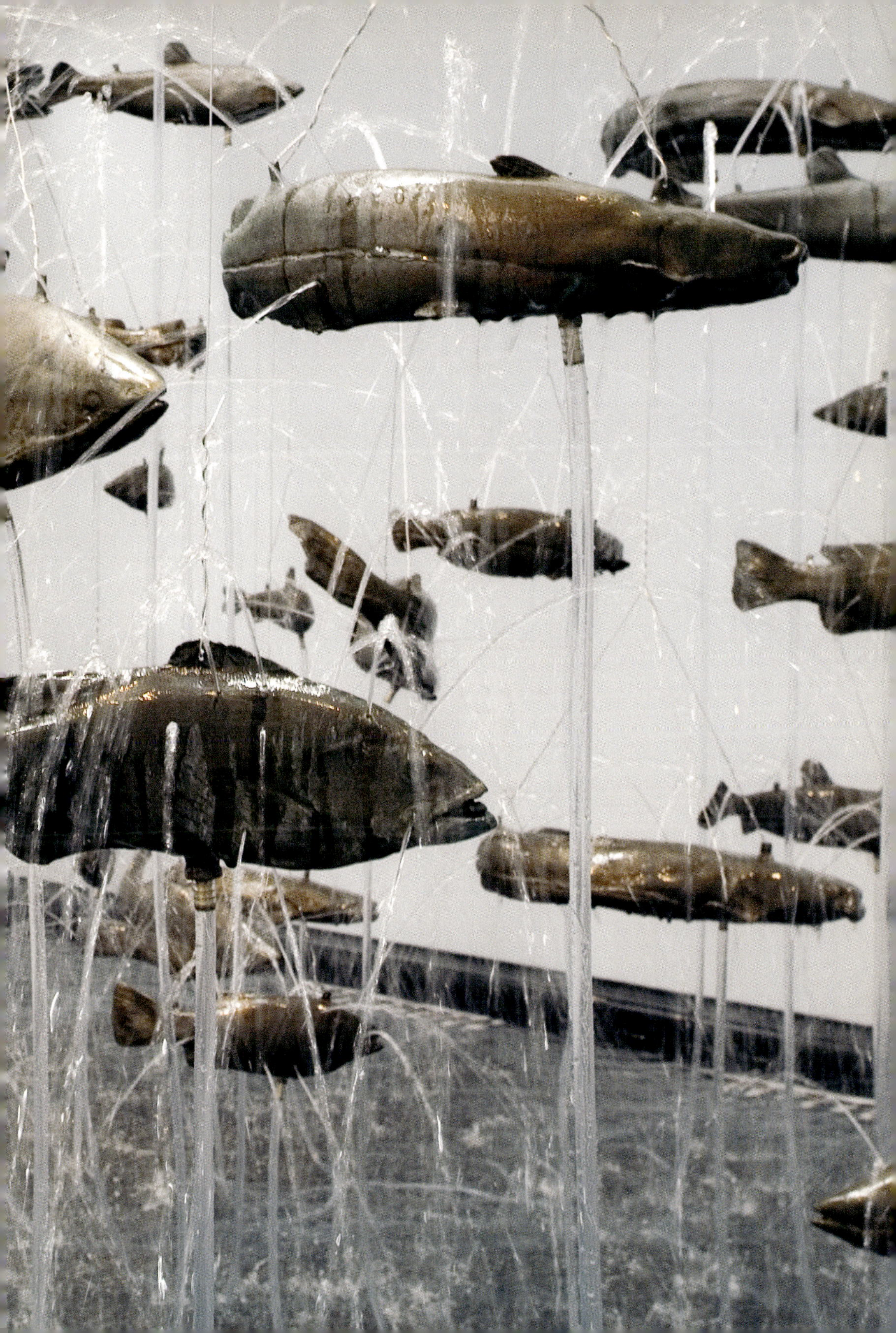

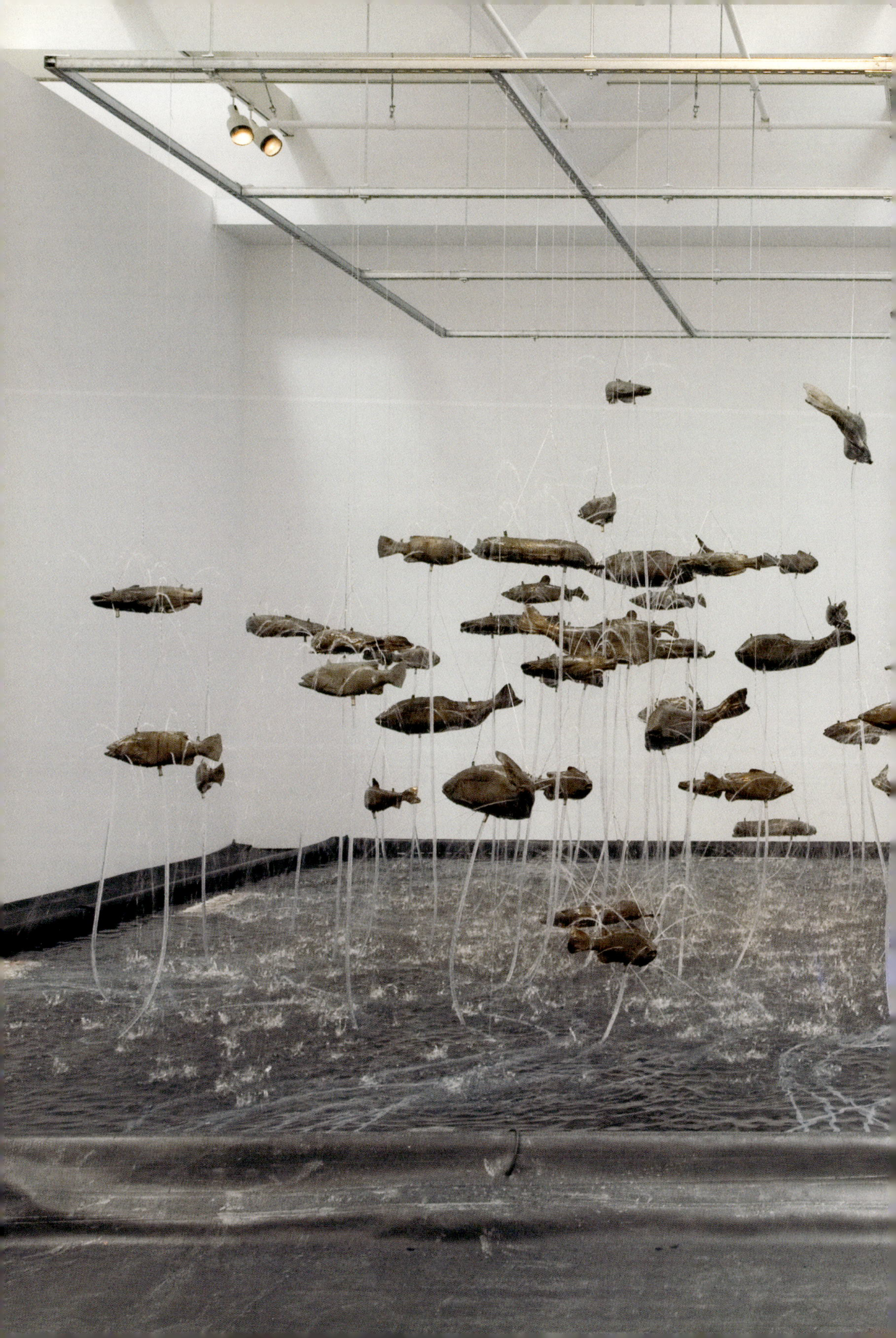

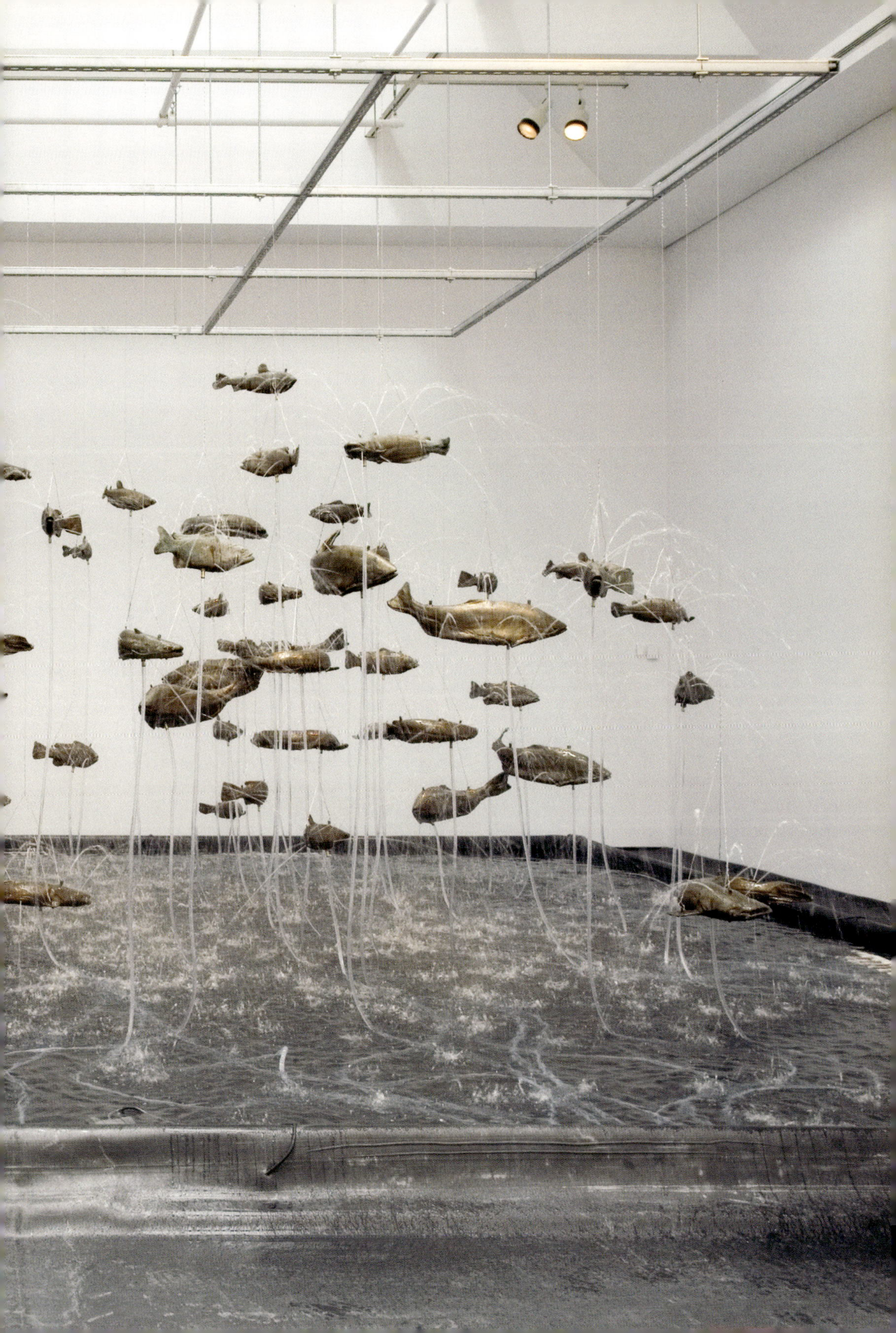

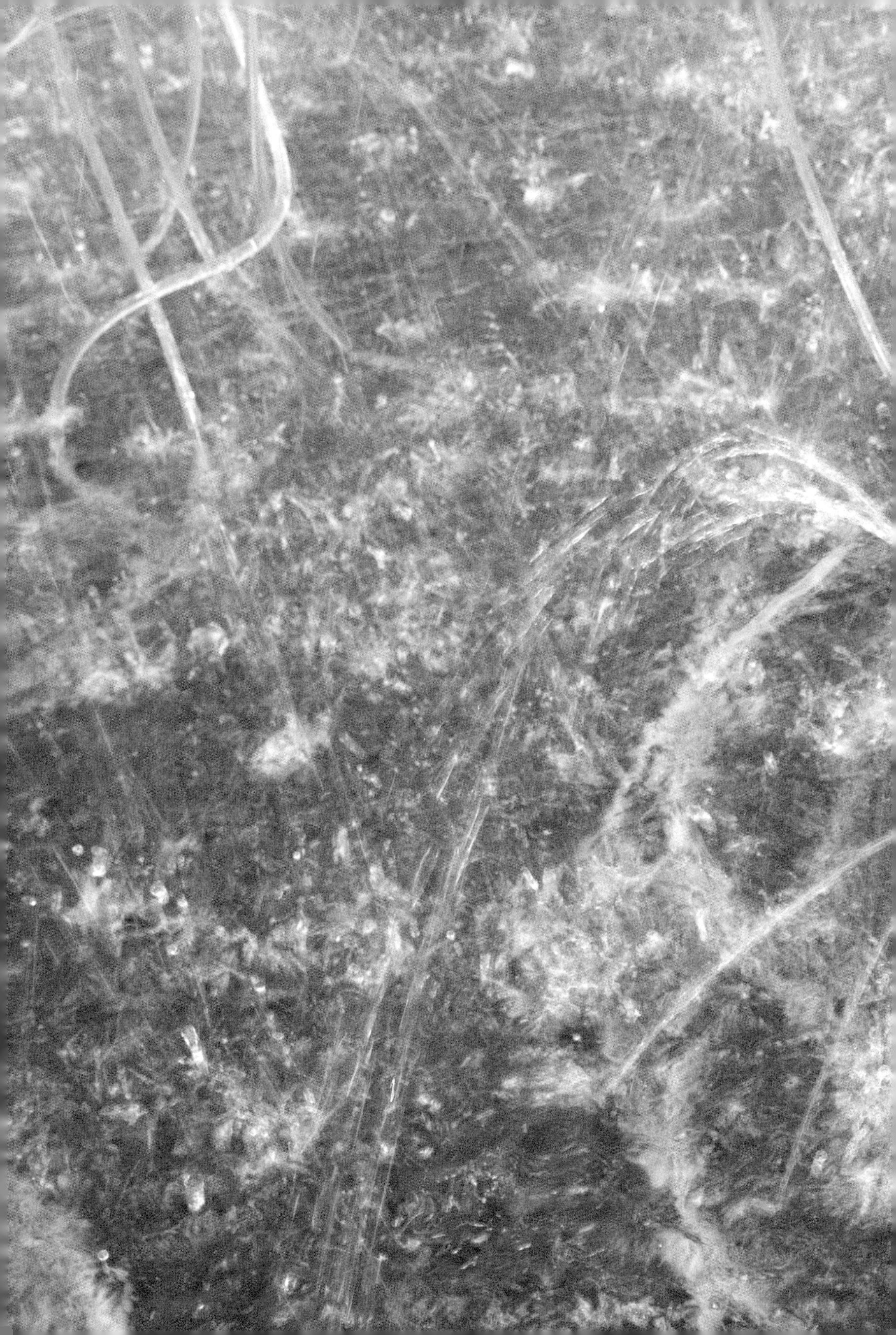

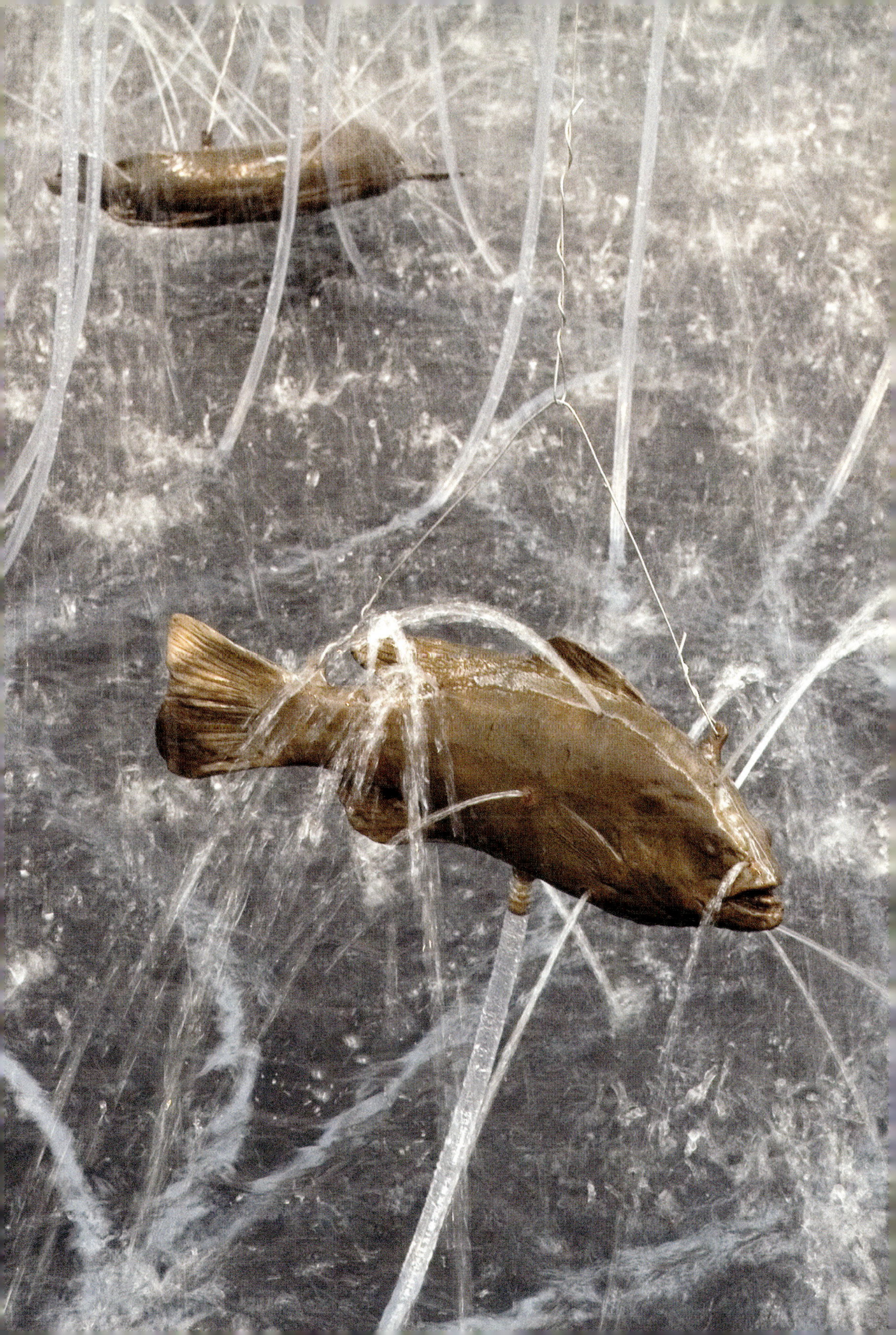

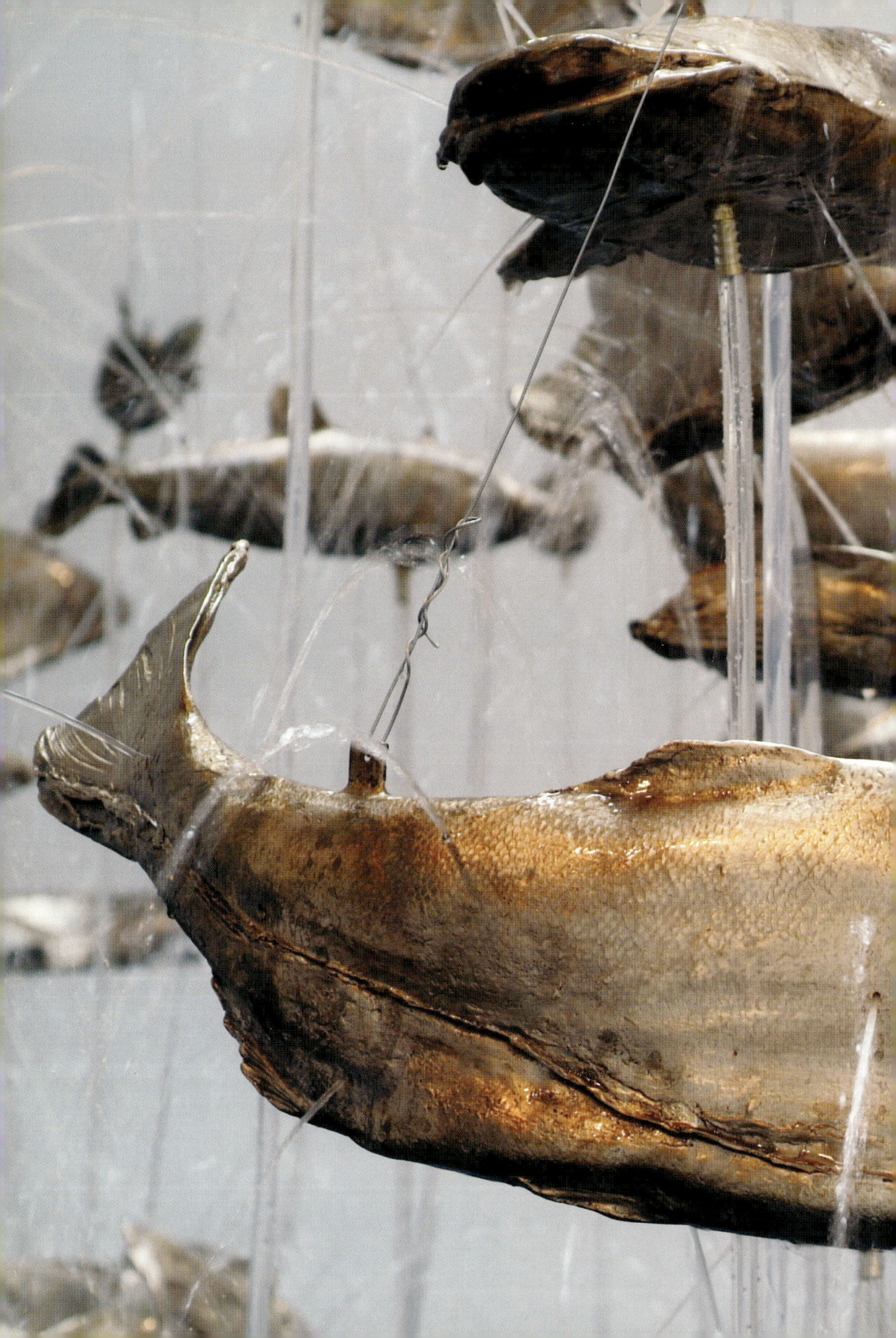

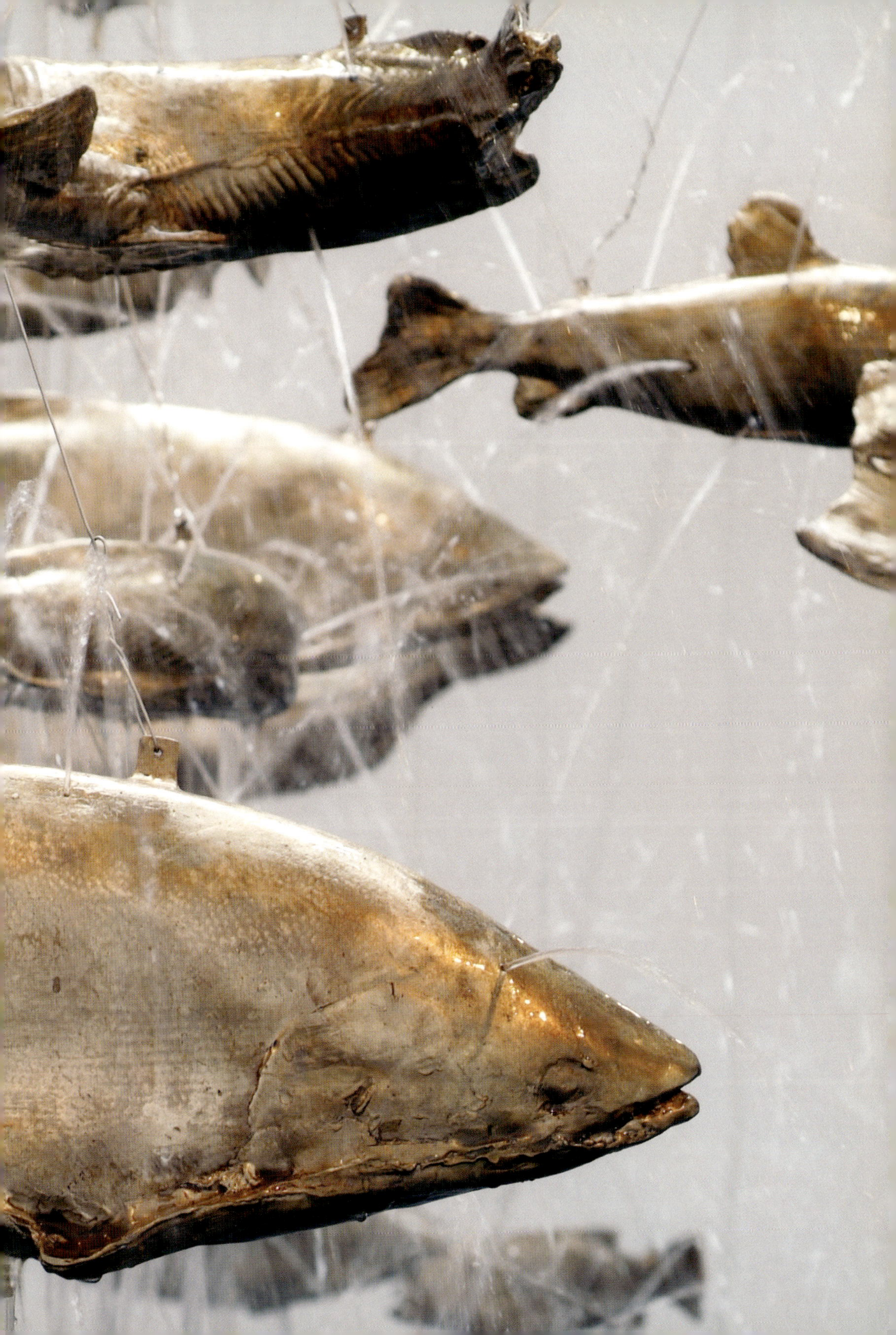

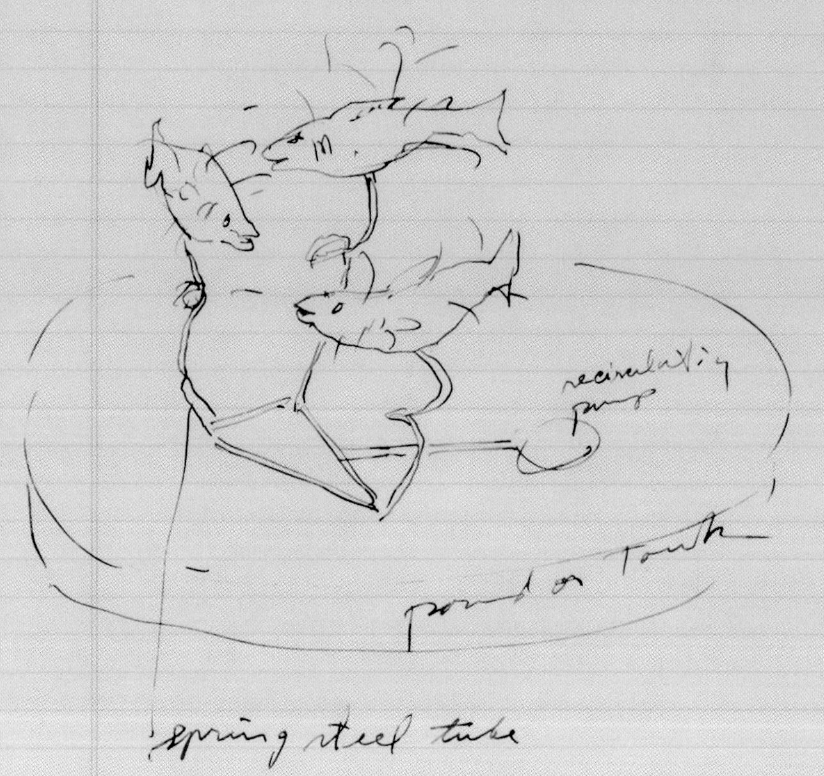

B Munro 04

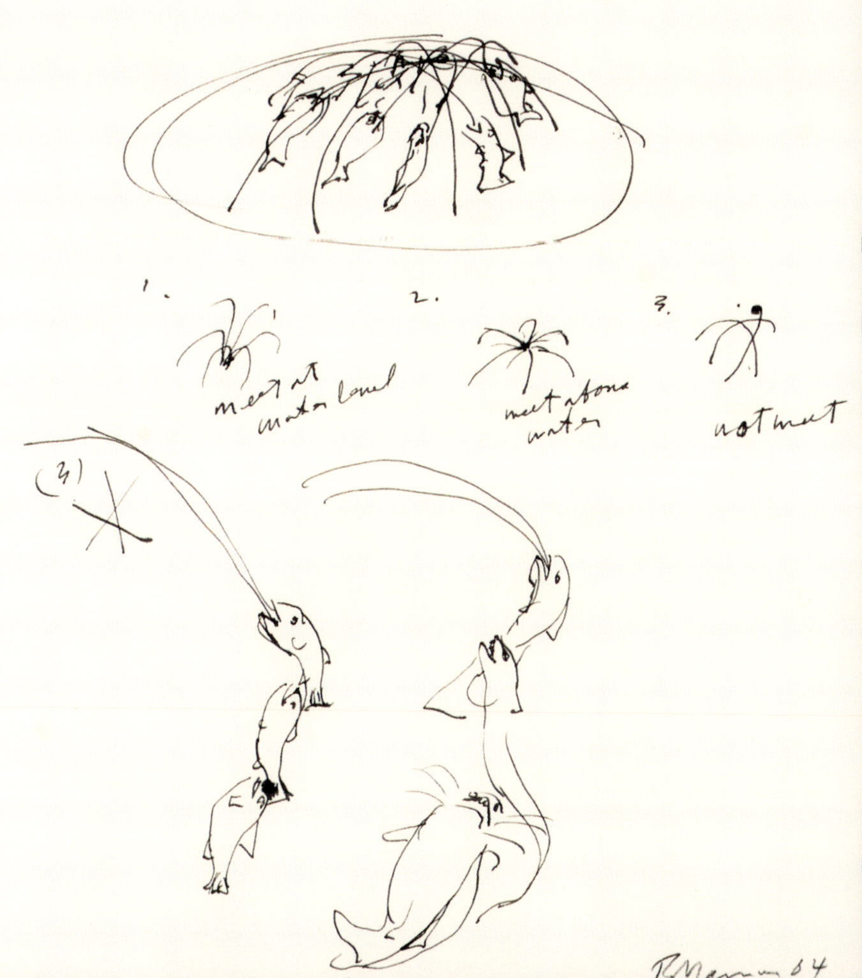

Fish Fountain
1. meet at water level
2. meet above water
3. not met
(3)
R Marcus 64

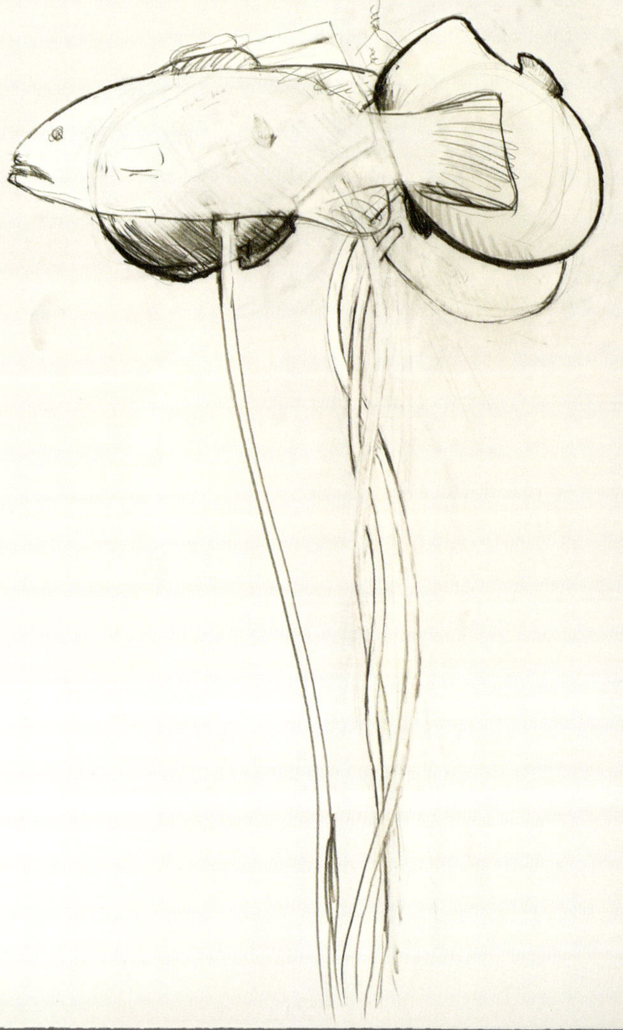

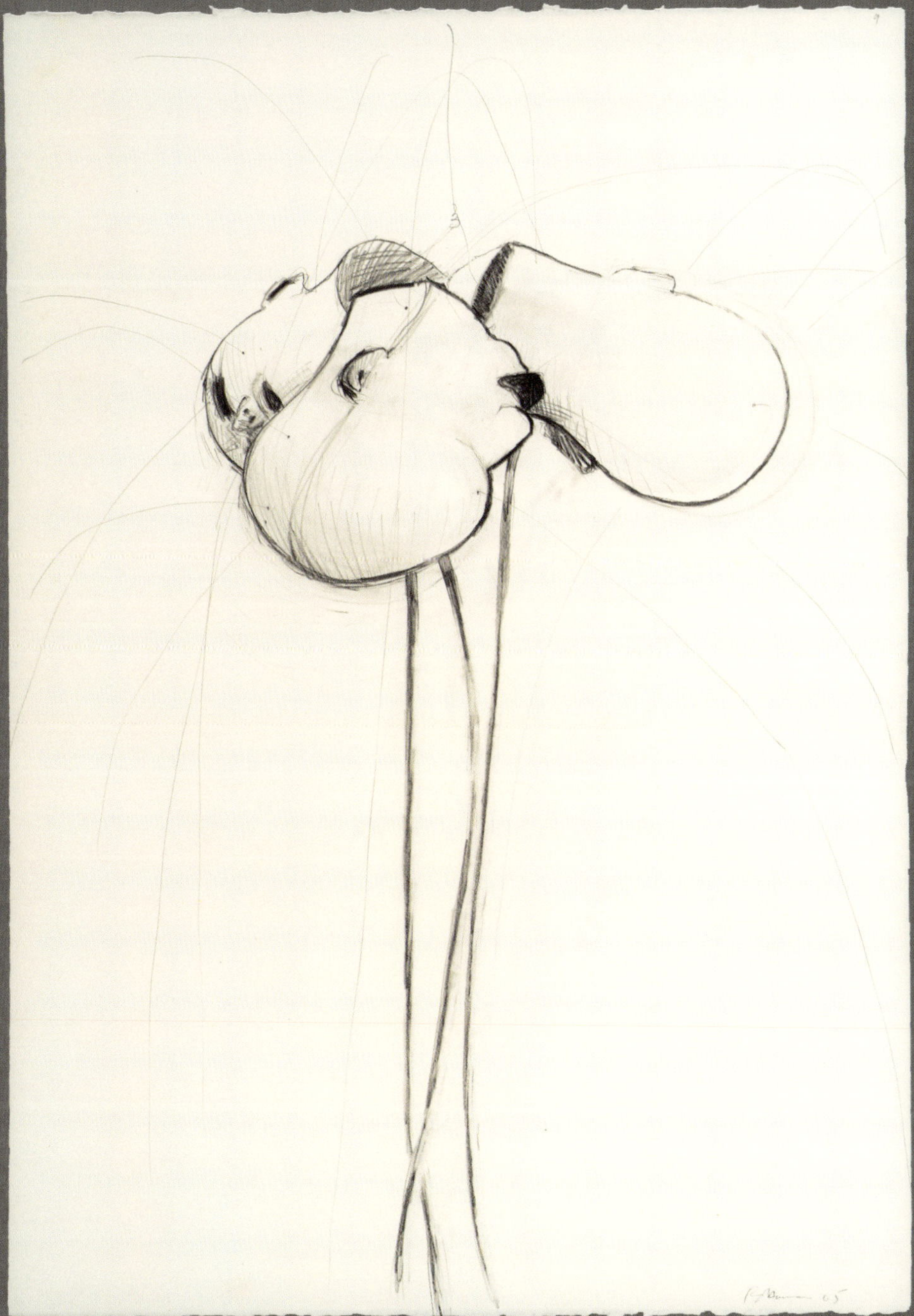

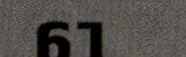

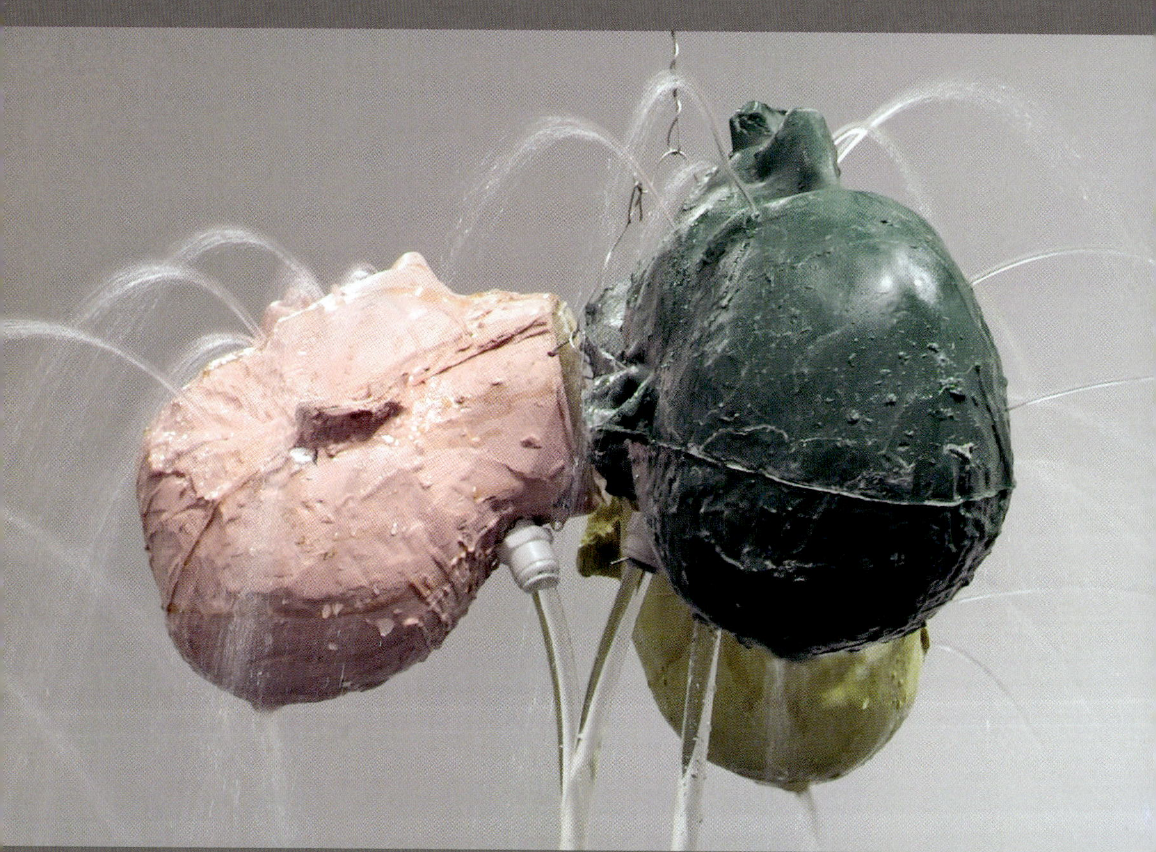

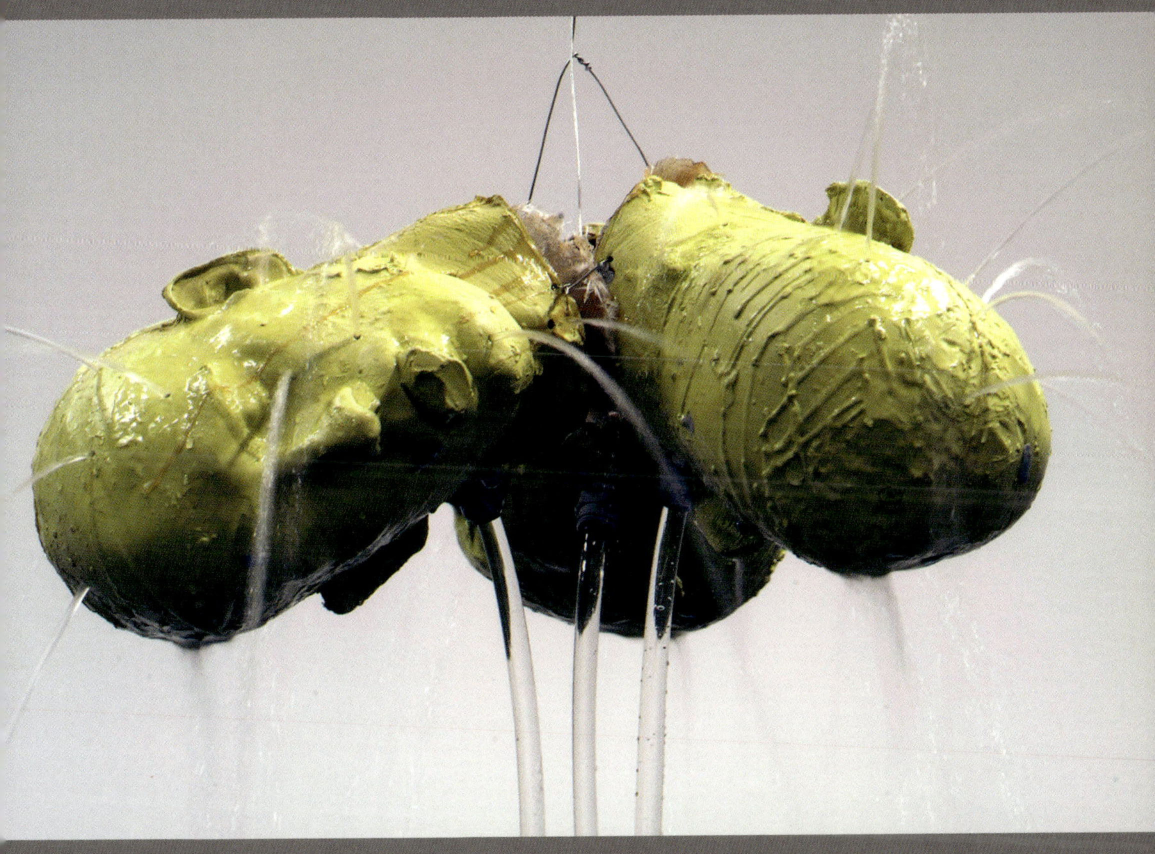

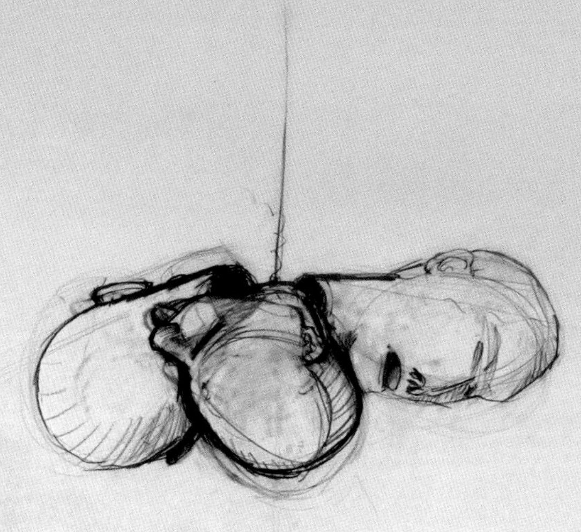

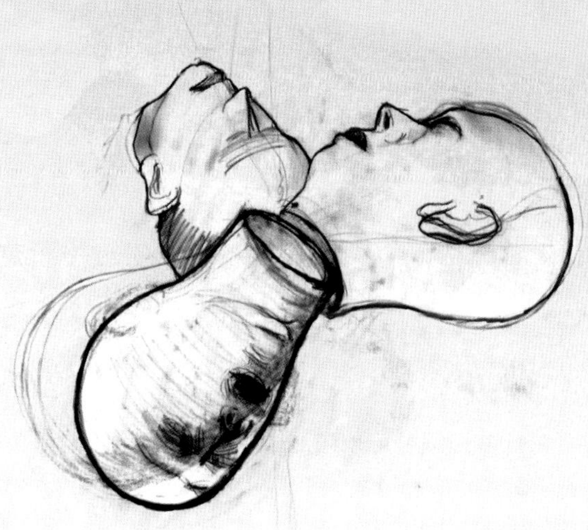

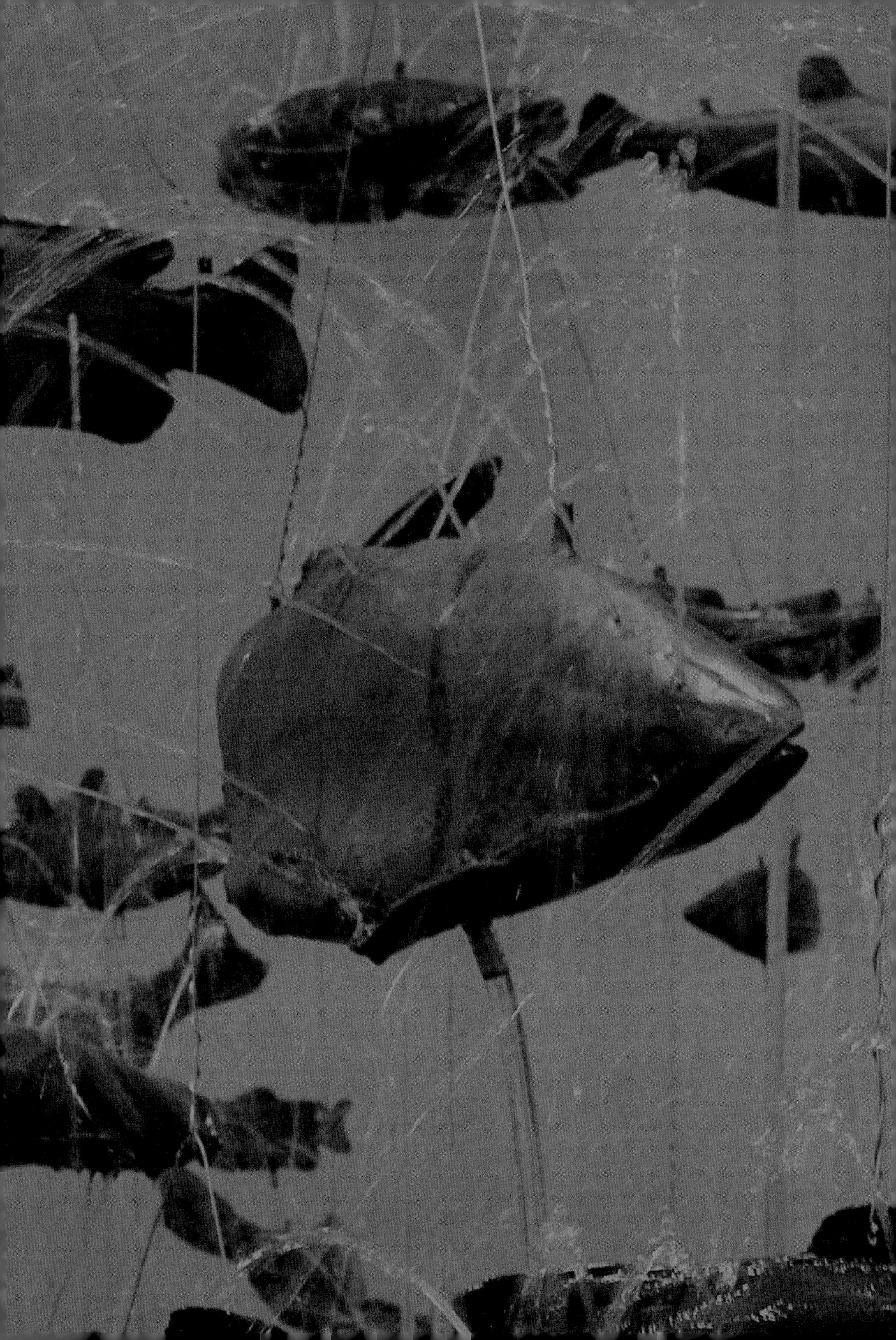

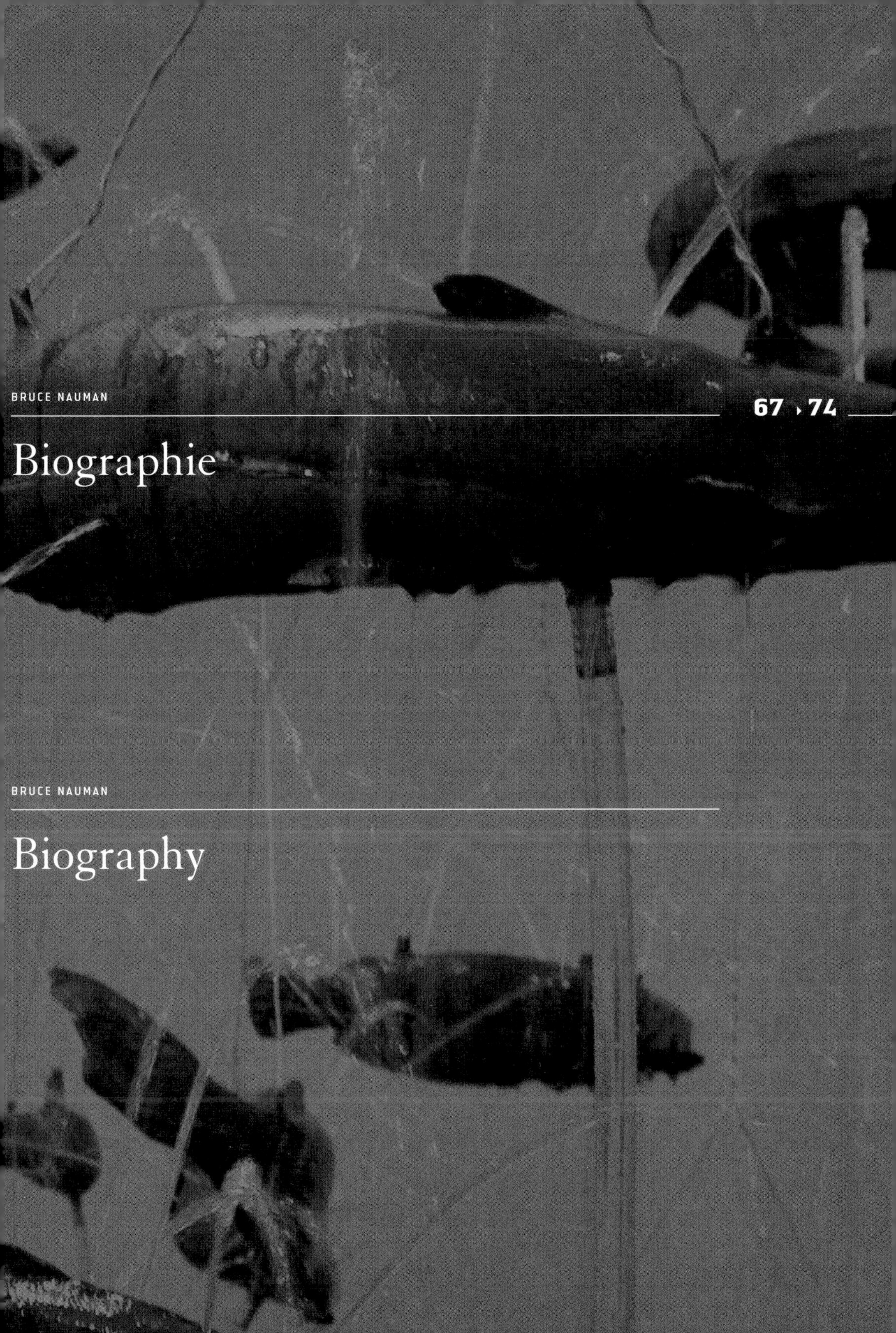

67 › 74

Biographie

BRUCE NAUMAN

Biography

1941 ▸ Bruce Nauman wird am 6. Dezember 1941 in Fort Wayne, Indiana geboren. Früh erhält er Klavier- und Gitarrenunterricht ....

1960 ▸ Er studiert Mathematik und Physik im Hauptfach und Kunst im Nebenfach an der Universität von Wisconsin, Madison, wo er 1964 seinen Abschluss macht. Fortan beschäftigt er sich mit Philosophie, speziell mit den Schriften Ludwig Wittgensteins ....

1964 ▸ Er nimmt sein Studium der Bildenden Künste an der University of California, Davis bei Robert Arneson und William T. Wiley wieder auf. Nauman wendet sich von der traditionellen Malerei ab und befasst sich mit prozessorientierten Skulpturen, Film, Video und photographischen Performances. Er wird Assistent von Wayne Thiebaud...............

1965 ▸ Zum ersten Mal stellt er ein komplettes Werkverzeichnis zusammen, das seine Skulpturen aus Fiberglas und Polyresin, Zeichnungen und Filme umfasst...............

1966 ▸ Nauman beendet sein Studium mit dem »Master of Fine Arts«. Er zieht um und beginnt seine Lehrtätigkeit am San Francisco Art Institute. Seine erste Einzelausstellung hat er in der Nicholas Wilder

1941 ▸ Bruce Nauman is born on December 6th, 1941, in Fort Wayne, IN. Early on, he receives piano and guitar lessons ....

1960 ▸ He majors in Mathematics and Physics and minors in Fine Arts at the University of Wisconsin, Madison, there he earns his degree in 1964. From now he engages in philosophy, predominantly in the writings of Ludwig Wittgenstein...............

1964 ▸ Once again, he takes up his studies in Fine Arts at the University of California, Davis, under Robert Arneson and William T. Wiley. Nauman turns away from traditional painting and gets involved in process-oriented sculptures and film, video and photography performances. He becomes Wayne Thiebaud's assistant ....

1965 ▸ For the first time, he compiles a catalog raisonné including sculptures made of fibreglass and poly-resin, drawings and films ....

1966 ▸ Nauman finishes his studies with a »Master of Fine Arts.« He moves and accepts a teaching position at the San Francisco Art Institute. He has his first solo exhibition at the Nicholas Wilder Gallery in Los

Gallery in Los Angeles. Er nimmt Teil an der Gruppenausstellung *Eccentric Abstraction* in der Fischbach Gallery in New York. Erste Filme mit William Allen, Neonarbeiten, Photographien, Arbeiten mit Körperabdrücken und Wortarbeiten enstehen ....
1968 ▸ Erste große Einzelausstellung in New York in der Leo Castelli Galery und erste Einzelausstellung in Europa in der Konrad Fischer Galerie, Düsseldorf. Einladung zur *documenta 4* in Kassel, wo er bis 1992 regelmässig vertreten sein wird (mit Ausnahme der *documenta 8*). Er entwirft Liveperformances für Schauspieler und Tänzer ....
1969 ▸ Umzug nach Pasadena, Kalifornien. Videoperformances, in denen Nauman als Hauptdarsteller auftritt, erreichen ihren Höhepunkt und finden gleichzeitig ihr vorläufiges Ende. Zum ersten Mal zeigt er Korridore, die normalerweise als Requisiten für Videoperformances benutzt wurden, als eigenständige Arbeiten in der Ausstellung *Anti-Illusions: Procedures/Materials* im Whitney Museum of American Art, New York. Er entwirft das Bühnenbild für das Tanzstück *Tread* der Merce Cunningham Dance Company. Erste closed-circuit Installationen: *Video Corridor for San Francisco (Come Piece)*..

Angeles and participates in the group exhibition *Eccentric Abstraction* at the Fischbach Gallery in New York. First films with William Allen, neon works, photographies, works with body molds, language and speech come into being ....
1968 ▸ First solo exhibition in New York at the Leo Castelli Gallery and first European solo exhibition at the Konrad Fischer Gallery, Duesseldorf. Invitation to *documenta 4* in Kassel in which he is represented regulary until 1992 (with the exception of *documenta 8*). He designs live performances for actors and dancers ....
1969 ▸ Relocation to Pasadena, CA. Video performances in which Nauman appears as the protagonist reach their climaxes and at the same time are brought to a temporary termination. For the first time corridors which were originally used as props for video performances are shown as independent works in the exhibition *Anti-Illusions: Procedures/Materials* at the Whitney Museum of American Art, New York. He designs the stage setting for the dance program *Tread* by the Merce Cunningham Dance Company. First closed circuit installations: *Video Corridor for San Francisco (Come Piece)* ....

1970 ▸ Unterrichtet Bildhauerei an der University of California, Irvine. Er befasst sich eingehend mit *Masse und Macht* (1962) von Elias Canetti und den Auswirkungen des privaten und öffentlichen Raums auf menschliche Verhaltensweisen...

1972 ▸ Das Los Angeles County Museum of Art und das Whitney Musuem of American Art, New York konzipieren die Wanderausstellung *Bruce Nauman. Work from 1965 to 1972*, die durch die USA und Europa tourt. Es ist die erste Ausstellung seiner Arbeiten in einem Museum ....

1973 ▸ Die vorerst letzten Videoperformances entstehen: unter anderem die Arbeit *Elke Allowing the Floor to Rise up Over Her, Face Up*. Die Beschäftigung mit Räumen, Sprache und Wortspielen wird immer wichtiger

1977 ▸ Erste Teilnahme an der Whitney Biennale (ebenso wie 1985, 1987, 1991 und 1997) ....

1978 ▸ Erste Teilnahme an der Biennale von Venedig (so auch 1980, 1999, 2005 und 2007)........................

1979 ▸ Umzug nach Pecos, New Mexico, wo er beginnt, sich intensiv mit Pferdedressur zu beschäftigen.

1981 ▸ Als Folge seiner Rauminstallationen entwickelt er große Hängeskulpturen der *South America* und *South Africa* Serie (Musical Chairs) ....

1970 ▸ Teaches Sculpture at the University of California, Irvine. He is concerned with into *Crowds and Power* (1962) by Elias Canetti and the impact of the private and the public sphere on human behaviour ....

1972 ▸ The Los Angeles County Museum of Art and the Whitney Museum of American Art, New York, conceive the travelling exhibition *Bruce Nauman. Work from 1965 to 1972* which tours through the U.S. and Europe. It is the first exhibition of his work in a museum..

1973 ▸ Last video performances for the time being develop: among others, the work *Elke Allowing the Floor to Rise up Over Her, Face Up* is produced. The occupation with spatial works, speech and puns becomes more and more important ....

1977 ▸ First participation in the Whitney Biennial (as well as 1985, 1987, 1991 and 1997) ....

1978 ▸ First participation in the Venice Biennial (as well as 1980, 1999, 2005 and 2007)........................

1979 ▸ Relocation to Pecos, NM, where he intensely starts engaging in horse dressage...........................

1981 ▸ As a sequel to his space installations he develops large overhead sculptures of the *South American* and *South African* set (Musical Chairs)...

1985 ▸ Ausstellung der Trilogie *Chambres d'Amis* im Haus Esters und Haus Lange, Krefeld bestehend aus folgenden Teilen: *Good Boy Bad Boy* (erste Videoarbeit seit 1973), *Hanged Man* (eine der ersten figuralen Neonarbeiten seit Mitte der 1960er Jahre) und *One Hundred Live and Die* (Soundarbeit)..............................

1986 ▸ Das Werkverzeichnis von Naumans Zeichnungen wird herausgegeben..

1987 ▸ Erste Videos mit Clowns als Akteuren entstehen ....

1988 ▸ Zum ersten Mal werden Tiere zu zentralen Motiven in Videos und Skulpturen. Der Film *Green Horse*, eine Zusammenarbeit mit der Choreographin Margaret Jenkins und dem Komponisten Terry Allen, zeigt Nauman, wieder einmal als Hauptdarsteller, wie er auf einem seiner Pferde reitet ....

1989 ▸ Das Werkverzeichnis von Naumans Druckgrafik wird publiziert. Er erhält die Ehrendoktorwürde des San Francisco Art Intitutes. Er entdeckt die Wachsköpfe als Thema.............................   ....

1990 ▸ Umzug in den Norden von New Mexico. Er erhält den *Max-Beckmann-Preis* der Stadt Frankfurt am Main. Die Arbeit *Raw Material – Brrr* wird realisiert und leitet eine Reihe von Videoinstallationen ein, in denen Nauman wieder regelmäßig als Darsteller auftritt ....

1985 ▸ Exhibition of the trilogy *Chambres d'Amis* at Haus Esters and Haus Lange, Krefeld, Germany, consisting of the following fragments: *Good Boy Bad Boy* (first video work since 1973), *Hanged Man*, one of the first neon works displaying figures since the mid-sixties and *One Hundred Live and Die* (sound work)

1986 ▸ The catolog raisonné of Nauman's drawings is being published ....

1987 ▸ First videos with clowns as protagonists come into being...

1988 ▸ For the first time, animals become central motives in videos and sculptures. The film *Green Horse*, a collaboration with the choreographer Margaret Jenkins and the composer Terry Allen, shows Nauman, back again as the protagonist, riding one of his horses ....

1989 ▸ The catalog raisonné of Nauman's graphic prints is being published. He receives the honorary doctorate at the San Francisco Art Institute. He discovers the wax heads as a theme ....

1990 ▸ Relocation to Northern New Mexiko. He receives the *Max-Beckmann-Preis* from the the city of Frankfurt, Main, Germany. The work *Raw Material – Brrr* is being realized and heralds a set of video installations in which Nauman appears as an actor regularly again...

1993 ▸ Das Walker Art Center in Minneapolis und das Hirshhorn Museum and Sculpture Garden in Washington D.C. organisieren eine große Bruce Nauman Retrospektive, die später im Museo Nacional Centro de Arte Reina Sofía, Madrid, dem Museum of Contemporary Art, Los Angeles und dem Museum of Modern Art, New York gezeigt wird. Nauman erhält den *Wolf* Preis für Bildende Kunst und Bildhauerei in Herzlia, Israel.
1994 ▸ Die Ohio State University verleiht ihm den *Wexner* Preis. Sein Werk konzentriert sich zu dieser Zeit auf Handabgüsse und architektonische Arbeiten im Außenraum...
1999 ▸ Zusammen mit Louise Bourgeois wird ihm für sein Lebenswerk der *Goldene Löwe* der 48. Biennale von Venedig verliehen..
2000 ▸ Er wird Mitglied der American Academy of Arts and Letters, New York und wird zum Ehrendoktor des California Institute of the Arts, Valencia ernannt...

1993 ▸ The Walker Art Center, Minneapollis, the Hirshhorn Museum and the Smithsonian Institution Washington D.C. organize a large Bruce Nauman retrospective which is later shown in the Museo Nacional Centro de Arte Reina Sofia in Madrid, the Museum of Contemporary Art in Los Angeles and the Museum of Modern Art in New York. Nauman receives the *Wolf* Prize for Fine Arts and Sculpture in Herzlia, Israel.
1994 ▸ Nauman is awarded the *Wexner* Prize by Ohio State University. At this point, his work is focused on molds of hands and architectual works in outdoor spaces ....
1999 ▸ Along with Louise Bourgeois, he is awarded the *Golden Lion* for his lifework at the 48th Venice Biennial ....
2000 ▸ He becomes a member of the American Academy of Arts and Letters, New York and is appointed honorary doctor at the California Institute of the Arts, Valencia ....

2004 ▸ Die Tate Modern, London bittet ihn, im Rahmen der Unilever Serie *(The Unilever Series)*, die gigantische Turbinenhalle der Tate Modern zu bespielen ....

2006 ▸ Nauman erhält als erster Künstler den neugeschaffenen *Düsseldorfer Kunstpreis*.............................

2007 ▸ Anlässlich der *Skulptur Projekte* Münster realisiert er die Arbeit *Square Depression*, die bereits 1977 anlässlich der ersten *Skulptur Projekte* geplant war, aber damals nicht durchgeführt werden konnte. Das Musée d'Art Contemporain de Montréal widmet seinem Werk eine große Ausstellung, in der auch *One Hundred Fish Fountain* gezeigt wird ....

Der Künstler lebt und arbeitet im Norden von New Mexico...

ZUSAMMENGESTELLT VON KATHARINA MISCHOK, ÜBERSETZT VON SARAH STEINGRUBE ....

2004 ▸ In the context of the *Unilever Series,* Tate Modern, London, asks him to arrange its gigantic Turbine Hall..

2006 ▸ As the first artist, Nauman is awarded the newly introduced *Düsseldorfer Kunstpreis*.....................

2007 ▸ On the occasion of *Sculpture Projects* Muenster Nauman realizes the work *Square Depression* which had already been planned for the the first *Sculpture Projects* in 1977 but could not be executed then. The Musée d'Art Contemporain de Montréal organizes a large exhibition dedicated to his work in which, among other works, *One Hundred Fish Fountain* is shown..

The artist lives and works in Northern New Mexico...

COMPILED BY KATHARINA MISCHOK, TRANSLATED BY SARAH STEINGRUBE...

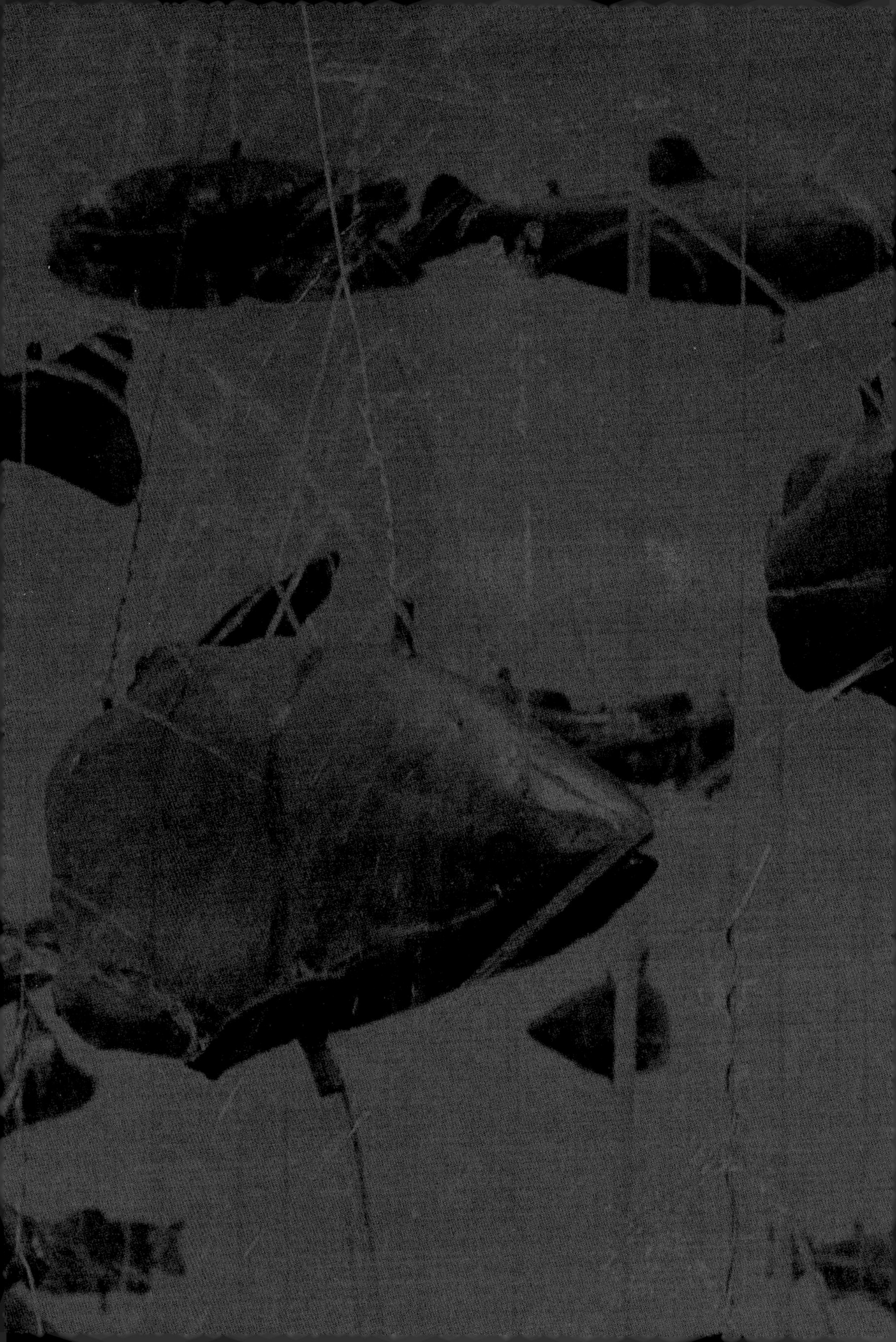

Bibliographie

Bibliography

A ROSE HAS NO TEETH: BRUCE NAUMAN IN THE 1960S. Texte von Constance M. Lewallen, Anne M. Wagner, Robert Storr und Robert R. Riley. Berkeley Art Museum und Pacific Film Archive, The Castello di Rivoli Museo d'Arte Contemporanea, Turin, Menil Collection, Houston 2007...

ELUSIVE SIGNS: BRUCE NAUMAN WORKS WITH LIGHT. (Ausst.-Kat.), Texte von Joseph D. Ketner II, Janet Kraynak und Gregory Volk. Indianapolis Museum of Art, Indianapolis, The MIT Press. 2006..................

BRUCE NAUMAN: MAKE ME THINK ME. Texte von Anna Dezeuze, Johanna Drucker, Lynne Cook und Laurence Sillars (Hrsg.). London 2006...

OPEN SYSTEMS: RETHINKING ART C. 1970. (Ausst.-Kat.), Tate Modern, De Salvo, Donna (Hrsg.). London 2005.

BRUCE NAUMAN: THE UNILEVER SERIES: RAW MATERIAL. ((Ausst.-Kat.), Tate Modern, Dexter, Emma (Hrsg.). London 2004...

BRUCE NAUMAN. THEATERS OF EXPERIENCE. (Ausst.-Kat.), Deutsche Guggenheim, Berlin. Berlin 2003............

AC: BRUCE NAUMAN. MAPPING THE STUDIO. (Fat Chance John Cage). (Ausst.-Kat.), Museum Ludwig, Köln. Texte von Kaspar König, Christine Litz und Beitr. des Künstlers. Köln 2003......................................

PLEASE PAY ATTENTION PLEASE: BRUCE NAUMAN'S WORDS: WRITINGS AND INTERVIEWS. Texte von Bruce Nauman, Janet Kraynak und Curtis Roads. Boston 2003..

SAMUEL BECKETT | BRUCE NAUMAN. (Ausst.-Kat.), Kunsthalle Wien, Wien. Texte von Gerald Matt, Sabine Folie, Christine Hoffmann, Michael Glasmeier, Joan Simon, Gaby Hartel, Friederike Wappler, Raymond Federman, Steven Connor, Kathryn Chiong, Hédy Kaddour, Werner Spies, Nam June Paik. Wien 2000....................

BRUCE NAUMAN. (Ausst.-Kat.), Wilhelm Lehmbruck Museum, Duisburg. Texte von Christoph Brockhaus, Ortrud Westheider, Gottlieb Leinz, Friederike Wappler, Ursula Frohne. Duisburg 2000.............................

BRUCE NAUMAN. (Ausst.-Kat.), Museum für Neue Kunst, ZKM Karlsruhe, Texte von Dörte Zbikowski, Reto Krüger, Ellen Heider, Ralph Melcher. Karlsruhe 1999 ....

BRUCE NAUMAN: DER WAHRE KÜNSTLER. THE TRUE ARTIST. Texte von Beatrice von Bismarck. Ostfildern 1998

BRUCE NAUMAN: VERSUCHSANORDNUNGEN. WERKE 1965–1994. (Ausst.-Kat.), Hamburger Kunsthalle. Texte von Uwe M. Schneede, Joan Simon, Barbara Engelbach, Melitta Kliege, Günter Metken, Friederike Wappler. Hamburg 1998...

BRUCE NAUMAN: IMAGE|TEXT 1966–1996. (Ausst.-Kat.), Kunstmuseum Wolfsburg 1997; Centre Georges Pompidou Mnam-Cci, Paris 1997; Hayward Gallery, London 1998; Taiteen museo of Contemporary Art, Helsinki 1998. Texte von Jean-Charles Masséra, Vincent Labaume, François Albera, Gijs van Tuyl, Christine

van Assche, Artikel von Marcia Tucker, Willoughby Sharp, Chris Dercon, Joan Simon, Tony Oursler und Michele De Angelus. Wolfsburg 1997 ....

BRUCE NAUMAN. 1985–1996. DRAWINGS, PRINTS AND RELATED WORKS. (Ausst.-Kat.), The Aldrich Museum of Contemporary Art, 1997. Synder, Jill (Hrsg.), The Cleveland Center of Contemporary Art 1998 ....

BRUCE NAUMAN: WORLD PEACE (PROJECTED). (Ausst.-Kat.), Staatsgalerie Moderner Kunst, München. Texte von Carla Schulz-Hoffmann und Peter Prange, München 1997 ....

BRUCE NAUMAN: INTERVIEWS, 1967–1988. Verlag der Kunst, Christine Hoffmann (Hrsg.), Amsterdam 1996

BRUCE NAUMAN: ELLIOTT'S STONES. (Ausst.-Kat.), Museum of Contemporary Art, Text von Lucinda Barnes, Chicago 1995 ....

BRUCE NAUMAN. (Ausst.-Kat. und Werkverzeichnis), Museo Nacional Centro de Arte Reina Sofia, Madrid, Walker Art Center, Minneapolis; Museum of Contemporary Art, Los Angeles, Hirshhorn Museum and Sculpture Garden, Smithsonian Institution, Washington, D.C., Museum of Modern Art, Texte von Neal Benezra, Kathy Halbreich, Paul Schimmel, Joan Simon und Robert Storr, New York 1994 ....

BRUCE NAUMAN: 25 YEARS, LEO CASTELLI. (Ausst.-Kat.), Leo Castelli Gallery, Brundage, Susan (Hrsg.). New York 1994 ....

BRUCE NAUMAN: SKULPTUREN UND INSTALLATIONEN, 1985–1990. (Ausst.-Kat.) Museum für Gegenwartskunst, Basel. Mitherausgeber: DuMont Buchverlage, Texte von Jörg Zutter und Franz Meyer. Köln 1990 ....

BRUCE NAUMAN. (Ausst.-Kat.), Whitechapel Art Gallery, Texte von Jean-Christophe Ammann, Nicholas Serota und Joan Simon. London 1986 ....

BRUCE NAUMAN: DRAWINGS 1965–1986. (Ausst.-Kat. und Werkverzeichnis), Museum für Gegenwartskunst, Texte von Coosje van Bruggen, Dieter Koepplin und Franz Meyer. Basel 1986 ....

BRUCE NAUMAN: STADIUM PIECE, MUSICAL CHAIRS, DREAM PASSAGE. (Ausst.-Kat.), Museum Haus Esters, Text von Julian Heynen. Krefeld 1983 ....

BRUCE NAUMAN: NEONS. (Ausst.-Kat. und Werkverzeichnis), Baltimore Museum of Art, Text von Brenda Richardson. Maryland 1982 ....

BRUCE NAUMAN: WORK FROM 1965 TO 1972. (Ausst.-Kat.), Los Angeles County Museum of Art, Texte von Jane Livingston und Marcia Tucker. Los Angeles 1972 ....

BRUCE NAUMAN. (Ausst.-Kat.), Leo Castelli Gallery, Text von David Whitney. New York 1968 ....

ZUSAMMENGESTELLT VON CHRISTIANE AUTSCH ....

PUBLIKATION ANLÄSSLICH DER AUSSTELLUNG |
PUBLICATION TO ACCOMPANY THE EXHIBITION
Bruce Nauman, One Hundred Fish Fountain
KESTNERGESELLSCHAFT, HANNOVER
28. September – 4. November 2007 |
September 28 – November 4, 2007
HERAUSGEGEBEN VON | EDITED BY
Veit Görner und | and Frank-Thorsten Moll,
kestnergesellschaft, Hannover
TEXTE | TEXTS
Veit Görner, Frank-Thorsten Moll, Roland Meyer
ÜBERSETZUNG DEUTSCH-ENGLISCH |
TRANSLATION GERMAN-ENGLISH
George Frederic Takis, Sarah Steingrube
LEKTORAT | COPYEDITING
Barbara Soldner und | and Sarah Grimmer
GRAFISCHE GESTALTUNG UND SATZ |
GRAPHIC DESIGN AND TYPESETTING
Birgit Schmidt, WWW.BIRGIT-SCHMIDT.DE
GESAMTHERSTELLUNG | PRODUCTION
Kehrer Design Heidelberg

© 2007 Bruce Nauman
© 2007 kestnergesellschaft, Hannover,
Kehrer Verlag Heidelberg
und Autoren | and authors
ERSCHIENEN IM | PUBLISHED BY
Kehrer Verlag Heidelberg
WWW.KEHRERVERLAG.COM
WWW.ARTBOOKSHEIDELBERG.COM

BIBLIOGRAFISCHE INFORMATION DER DEUTSCHEN |
NATIONALBIBLIOTHEK
Die Deutsche Nationalbibliothek verzeichnet diese
Publikation in der Deutschen Nationalbibliografie;
detaillierte bibliografische Daten sind im Internet
über HTTP://DNB.D-NB.DE abrufbar.
BIBLIOGRAPHIC INFORMATION PUBLISHED BY THE |
DEUTSCHE NATIONALBIBLIOTHEK
The Deutsche Nationalbibliothek lists this publica-
tion in the Deutsche Nationalbibliografie; detailed
bibliographic data are available in the internet at
HTTP://DNB.D-NB.DE.

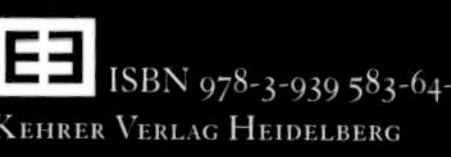 ISBN 978-3-939 583-64-6
Kehrer Verlag Heidelberg
Printed in Germany

UMSCHLAGABBILDUNG | COVER ILLUSTRATION
bruce nauman ▶ One Hundred Fish Fountain, 2005
▶ 97 bronze fish of seven different forms, suspended
with stainless steel wire from a metal grid | 97 bronzene
Fische in 7 unterschiedlichen Formen, an Stahldraht von
einem Gitter herabhängend, Detailansicht ▶ Approximate
basin dimensions: 8 in. h × 25 ft. × 28 ft. | ungefähre
Bassinmaße: 20,3 × 762 × 853,4 cm ▶ Installationview |
Installationsansicht: Musée d'Art Contemporain,
Montréal ▶ Foto: Richard-Max Tremblay ▶ Courtesy
Donald Young Gallery, Chicago ▶ Sender Collection,
New York ▶ VG Bildkunst, 2007

kestnergesellschaft
Goseriede 11
30159 Hannover
Germany
Fon +49 511 70120 0
Fax +49 511 70120 20
kestner@kestner.org
WWW.KESTNER.ORG

DIREKTOR | DIRECTOR
Veit Görner

AUSSTELLUNG | EXHIBITION
Frank-Thorsten Moll

STELLVERTRETENDE GESCHÄFTSFÜHRERIN |
DEPUTY GENERAL MANAGER
Mairi Kroll

KURATOREN | CURATORS
Eveline Bernasconi, Caroline Käding,
Frank-Thorsten Moll

PRESSE- UND ÖFFENTLICHKEITSARBEIT |
PUBLIC RELATIONS
Rebekka Maiwald

EMPFANG | FRONT DESK
Angela Pohl

RECHNUNGSWESEN | ACCOUNTING DEPARTMENT
Helga Dietrich, Petra Lücke

AUSSTELLUNGSTECHNIK, BETRIEBSTECHNIK |
INSTALLATION OF EXHIBITION, TECHNICAL RESOURCES
Jörg-Maria Brügger, Rainer Walter

MITGLIEDERVERWALTUNG | MEMBER ADMINISTRATION
Sabine Sauermilch

KESTNERLABOR | INTERNS
Christiane Autsch, Sarah Grimmer, Sabrina Hoff,
Bettina Lemburg, Rosa Mezzanotte, Elisabeth
Minewitsch, Katharina Mischok, Barbara Soldner,
Sarah Steingrube

ERWEITERTES TEAM | EXTENDED TEAM
Guido Bode, Vivica Bree, Sigrid Didjurgis, Christoph
Dirkes, Jürgen Fischer, Friederike Haeussler, Daniel
Henze, Dr. Brigitte Kirch, Robert Knoke, Eddie
Lange, Waltraut Meinecke, Johanna Meisner,
Germaine Mogg, Beatrix Nagy-Meier, Viktor Pfafenrot,
Carsten Schlaefke, Dorothee Schniewind, Vimol
Staroste, Christel Sternhagen, Michael Stoeber,
Irmela Wilckens

KESTNERCORPORATEPARTNER |
KESTNERCORPORATEPARTNERS
Innerstadt GmbH & Co. KG
HANNOVER Finanz
NORD/LB
Verlagsgesellschaft Madsack
VHV Versicherungen

KESTNERCORPORATEFÖRDERER |
KESTNERCORPORATEPATRONS
AWD
GP Papenburg Baugesellschaft mbH

KESTNERFIRMENPARTNER |
KESTNERCOMPANYPARTNERS
Architekten BKSP
ARS MUNDI
Deloitte & Touche
Deutsche Messe AG
Hannover Rück
Sparkasse Hannover

KESTNERFIRMENFÖRDERER |
KESTNERCOMPANYPATRONS
R. Claus Bingemer
Norbert Essing Kommunikation
Investa Projektentwicklungs- und Verwaltungs GmbH
B. Metzler seel. Sohn & Co.

IT PARTNER DER | OF KESTNERGESELLSCHAFT
FINANZ_IT

WEBPARTNER DER | OF KESTNERGESELLSCHAFT
Dievision

Die kestnergesellschaft wird durch das Land
Niedersachsen unterstützt | The kestnergesellschaft
is supported by the Federal State of Lower Saxony

DIE AUSSTELLUNG WIRD GEFÖRDERT DURCH |
THE EXHIBITION IS SUPPORTED BY
den Förderkreis der kestnergesellschaft |
the friends of the kestnergesellschaft

NORD/LB

STEINBERG.GÄRTEN

BESONDEREN DANK AN | SPECIAL THANKS TO
Bruce Nauman, Sandra Grant-Marchand, Klaus
Kehrer, Emily Letourneau, Todd Levin, Brennan
McGaffey, Juliet Myers, Birgit Schmidt, Lenore and
Adam Sender, Donald Young, Anne-Marie Zepettelli

Dieser Katalog wurde erst möglich durch die
grosszügige Unterstützung der Sender Collection,
New York | This catalogue has been made possible
only with the generous suppport of the Sender
Collection, New York

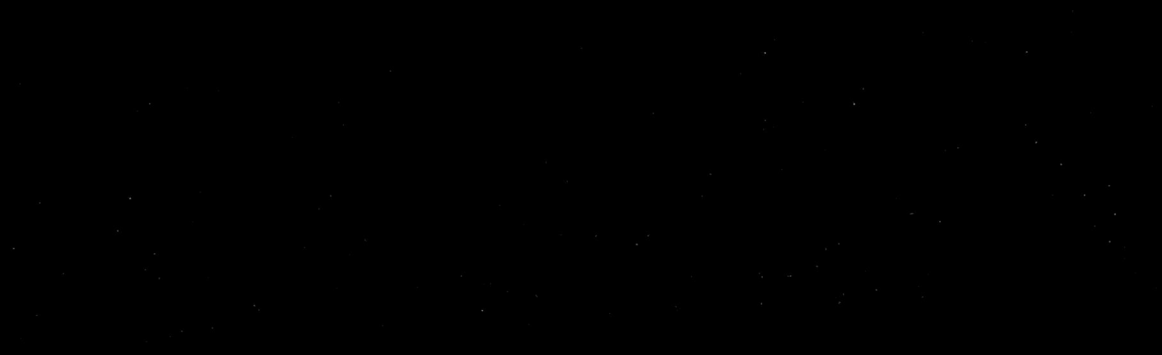

DIREKTOR | DIRECTOR
Veit Görner
AUSSTELLUNG | EXHIBITION
Frank-Thorsten Moll
STELLVERTRETENDE GESCHÄFTSFÜHRERIN |
DEPUTY GENERAL MANAGER
Mairi Kroll
KURATOREN | CURATORS
Eveline Bernasconi, Caroline Käding,
Frank-Thorsten Moll
PRESSE- UND ÖFFENTLICHKEITSARBEIT |
PUBLIC RELATIONS
Rebekka Maiwald
EMPFANG | FRONT DESK
Angela Pohl
RECHNUNGSWESEN | ACCOUNTING DEPARTMENT
Helga Dietrich, Petra Lücke
AUSSTELLUNGSTECHNIK, BETRIEBSTECHNIK |
INSTALLATION OF EXHIBITION, TECHNICAL RESOURCES
Jörg-Maria Brügger, Rainer Walter
MITGLIEDERVERWALTUNG | MEMBER ADMINISTRATION
Sabine Sauermilch
KESTNERLABOR | INTERNS
Christiane Autsch, Sarah Grimmer, Sabrina Hoff,
Bettina Lemburg, Rosa Mezzanotte, Elisabeth
Minewitsch, Katharina Mischok, Barbara Soldner,
Sarah Steingrube
ERWEITERTES TEAM | EXTENDED TEAM
Guido Bode, Vivica Bree, Sigrid Didjurgis, Christoph
Dirkes, Jürgen Fischer, Friederike Haeussler, Daniel
Henze, Dr. Brigitte Kirch, Robert Knoke, Eddie
Lange, Waltraut Meinecke, Johanna Meisner,
Germaine Mogg, Beatrix Nagy-Meier, Viktor Pfafenrot,
Carsten Schlaefke, Dorothee Schniewind, Vimol
Staroste, Christel Sternhagen, Michael Stoeber,
Irmela Wilckens
KESTNERCORPORATEPARTNER |
KESTNERCORPORATEPARTNERS
Innerstadt GmbH & Co. KG
HANNOVER Finanz
NORD/LB
Verlagsgesellschaft Madsack
VHV Versicherungen

KESTNERCORPORATEFÖRDERER |
KESTNERCORPORATEPATRONS
AWD
GP Papenburg Baugesellschaft mbH
KESTNERFIRMENPARTNER |
KESTNERCOMPANYPARTNERS
Architekten BKSP
ARS MUNDI
Deloitte & Touche
Deutsche Messe AG
Hannover Rück
Sparkasse Hannover
KESTNERFIRMENFÖRDERER |
KESTNERCOMPANYPATRONS
R. Claus Bingemer
Norbert Essing Kommunikation
Investa Projektentwicklungs- und Verwaltungs GmbH
B. Metzler seel. Sohn & Co.
IT PARTNER DER | OF KESTNERGESELLSCHAFT
FINANZ_IT
WEBPARTNER DER | OF KESTNERGESELLSCHAFT
Dievision
Die kestnergesellschaft wird durch das Land
Niedersachsen unterstützt | The kestnergesellschaft
is supported by the Federal State of Lower Saxony
DIE AUSSTELLUNG WIRD GEFÖRDERT DURCH |
THE EXHIBITION IS SUPPORTED BY
den Förderkreis der kestnergesellschaft |
the friends of the kestnergesellschaft

NORD/LB

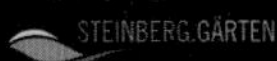

BESONDEREN DANK AN | SPECIAL THANKS TO
Bruce Nauman, Sandra Grant-Marchand, Klaus
Kehrer, Emily Letourneau, Todd Levin, Brennan
McGaffey, Juliet Myers, Birgit Schmidt, Lenore and
Adam Sender, Donald Young, Anne-Marie Zepettelli

Dieser Katalog wurde erst möglich durch die
grosszügige Unterstützung der Sender Collection,
New York | This catalogue has been made possible
only with the generous suppport of the Sender
Collection, New York